T0317334

CHILDREN'S VOICES, FAMILY DISPUTES AND CHILD-INCLUSIVE MEDIATION

Law, Society, Policy

Series Editor: **Rosie Harding**,
University of Birmingham

Law, Society, Policy offers an outlet for high quality, socio-legal research
monographs and edited collections with the potential for
policy impact.

Scan the code below to discover new and forthcoming titles in the series, or visit:

bristoluniversitypress.co.uk/law–society-policy

ANNE BARLOW AND JAN EWING

WITH A FOREWORD
BY GILLIAN DOUGLAS

CHILDREN'S VOICES, FAMILY DISPUTES AND CHILD-INCLUSIVE MEDIATION

The Right to Be Heard

BRISTOL
UNIVERSITY
PRESS

First published in Great Britain in 2024 by

Bristol University Press
University of Bristol
1–9 Old Park Hill
Bristol
BS2 8BB
UK
t: +44 (0)117 374 6645
e: bup-info@bristol.ac.uk

Details of international sales and distribution partners are available at
bristoluniversitypress.co.uk

British Library Cataloguing in Publication Data
A catalogue record for this book is available from the British Library

ISBN 978-1-5292-2891-5 paperback
ISBN 978-1-5292-2892-2 ePUB
ISBN 978-1-5292-2893-9 OA PDF

Cover design: Andrew Corbett
Front cover image: Andy Simpson Photography

Contents

Series Editor's Preface

The Law, Society, Policy series publishes high-quality, socio-legal research monographs and edited collections with the potential for policy impact.

Cutting across the traditional divides of legal scholarship, Law, Society, Policy offers an interdisciplinary, policy-engaged approach to socio-legal research which explores law in its social and political contexts with a particular focus on the place of law in everyday life.

The series seeks to take an explicitly society-first view of socio-legal studies, with a focus on the ways that law shapes social life, and the constitutive nature of law and society. International in scope, engaging with domestic, international and global legal and regulatory frameworks, texts in the Law, Society, Policy series engage with the full range of socio-legal topics and themes.

Table of Legislation

Bills

Children's Rights Bill 2009
Rights of the Child (Incorporation) (Scotland) Bill 2021

International conventions and treaties

European Convention on Human Rights
United Nations Convention on the Rights of the Child

Practice directions

Family Procedure Rules, Practice Direction 3A
Family Procedure Rules, Practice Direction 12B

Statutes

Children Act 1989
Children and Families Act 2014
Children (Scotland) Act 1995
Family Law Act 1996
Matrimonial Causes Act 1973
Rights of the Children and Young Persons (Wales) Measure 2011

List of Abbreviations

CA 1989	Children Act 1989
CIM	child-inclusive mediation
FJYPB	Family Justice Young People's Board
FMC	Family Mediation Council
HeaRE	*Healthy Relationship Education* study
HeaRT	*Healthy Relationship Transitions* study
LASPO	Legal Aid, Sentencing and Punishment of Offenders Act 2012
Mapping	*Mapping Paths to Family Justice* project
MIAM	Mediation and Information Assessment Meeting
NACCC	National Association of Child Contact Centres
NYAS	National Youth Advocacy Service
PSHE	personal, social, health and economic education
RE	relationship education
UNCRC	United Nations Convention on the Rights of the Child

About the Authors

Anne Barlow is Professor of Family Law and Policy at the University of Exeter Law School. She is a socio-legal researcher and has led a number of empirical research projects, including *Mapping Paths to Family Justice* and the recent *Healthy Relationship Transitions (HeaRT)* study on which this book draws. She has served as the Academic Member of the Family Justice Council (2011–15) and as a member of the government's Task Force on Family Mediation (2014). Her co-authored book, *Mapping Paths to Family Justice: Resolving Family Disputes in Neo-Liberal Times* (Palgrave, 2017) (with Rosemary Hunter, Janet Smithson and Jan Ewing) also won the Hart-SLSA book prize 2018.

Jan Ewing is Assistant Professor of Family Law at the University of Cambridge. From 2011 to 2023 she was a research fellow at the University of Exeter working with Anne Barlow on a number of projects including *Mapping* and then *Creating Paths to Family Justice*, an evaluation of the Department for Work and Pensions-funded *Mediation in Mind* project and more recently the *Healthy Relationship Transitions* project. She is a member of the Family Solutions Group, a multidisciplinary group of professionals set up by Sir Stephen Cobb in 2020 to consider what can be done to improve the experiences of children and families before an application is made to the family court.

Acknowledgements

We would like to express our enormous gratitude to all those who have helped make this book possible. First of all, our *HeaRT* study research participants – children, parents and professionals – who gave us their time and insights. This has enabled us to develop our understanding of the issues through exploring your different viewpoints and journeys involving child-inclusive mediation. You were, of course, all crucial to the success of the project, and we thank you again. The young people who took part in our focus groups and youth panels, as well as those who shared their experiences of mediation with us in interviews, were inspirational. They were also instrumental in reshaping our engaged methods during the COVID-19 lockdowns and co-creating our initial findings. The Family Justice Young People's Board, supported by Cafcass, were critical in helping us recruit young people nationally who had experienced parental separation and in supporting them in attending our group events. We are similarly greatly indebted to all the youth groups and schools in the South West of England, which agreed to invite their members to participate and to their dedicated leaders and staff who supported their attendance. We learned so much from you all and enjoyed the vibrancy of our discussions and debates, particularly in the final mixed youth panel. We also extend our huge thanks to the parents and children who had experienced child-inclusive mediation for being prepared to share your thoughts with us at what for many of you was a difficult time.

Next, we would like to sincerely thank all the relationship experts and family mediators who gave their time freely and provided crucial expertise which was fundamental to the study. We would not have got very far without your contributions. We are also thankful to the Family Mediation Council, its member organizations and members for their assistance in helping us to recruit our sample of parents and young people, without which the study would not have been possible.

Last but not least, we thank our funders, the Wellcome Trust-funded Wellcome Centre for Cultures and Environments of Health at the University of Exeter, and in particular, the Centre's administrative staff alongside our Medical School colleagues there, Simon Benham-Clarke and Tamsin Newlove-Delgado. Not only did they support, discuss and challenge our ideas, but also co-convened the online youth panels and supported different aspects of the study throughout.

Finally, we would like to make clear that all opinions expressed in this book are those of the authors, unless otherwise indicated. In addition, any errors and omissions are our own.

Foreword

Gillian Douglas
Emeritus Professor of Law,
Kings College London

During my career, I have been involved in several research projects exploring how children have experienced their parents' separation and divorce, including when they were caught up in legal proceedings between their parents in the family justice system. As part of these studies, information was gathered directly from children themselves. They spoke articulately and movingly about what it was like for them to live through their parents' break-up and how much they had wanted, and needed, to be consulted and involved in the arrangements their parents made to look after them after they separated.

Mediation has long been seen by policy makers as the preferred method of resolving family disputes where parents cannot do so themselves. The research undertaken in this book, exploring how child-inclusive mediation operates in England and Wales, and how it is experienced by parents and children as well as the professionals, is therefore an immensely valuable contribution to policy debates regarding the future direction of the family justice system and the place of child-inclusive processes within it.

The research is underscored by a firm commitment to the concept of children's rights and to the goal of incorporating the United Nations Convention on the Rights of the Child into domestic law. In harnessing this commitment to their study of mediation, Anne Barlow and Jan Ewing have provided us with a wealth of data as well as presenting a convincing argument for a move away from a focus on adult autonomy in decision-making towards a more relational approach which gives due weight to the perspectives of all involved – including the children. Such an approach holds the promise of bringing about a new and fairer vision of family justice, in all its forms.

ONE

Introduction

Background and aims

This book explores the law, theory and practice of family dispute resolution from a children's rights perspective. It has a particular focus on family mediation and its capacity to hear and listen to children's voices about child arrangements when parents separate. It is set in the context of a family justice system in England and Wales undergoing radical, neoliberal policy-driven reform, which strongly encourages mediation over court processes. However, until now, there has been much rhetoric but little evidence on what these reforms mean for children's experiences of parental separation. To help address this gap, our analysis here will draw on new empirical research from a Wellcome Trust Centre-funded project where, for the first time, children who had experienced child-inclusive mediation (CIM) and so were consulted separately by the mediator as part of their parents' family mediation process, were key research participants.

The policy rhetoric around family mediation in England and Wales has always proclaimed it as a process which is 'better for children'. Indeed, the government response to the *Family Justice Review* (Norgrove, 2011), which had first advocated the incorporation of family mediation as part of the family justice system, was subtitled *A System with Children and Families at its Heart* (Ministry of Justice (MoJ) and Department for Education (DfE), 2012a). Some children and young people were consulted as part of the *Family Justice Review* process, and a report aimed at children and young people, summarizing the recommendations, was also published (MoJ and DfE, 2012b). However, significantly, while the *Family Justice Review* had called for CIM to be available to 'all families seeking to mediate, provided that it is appropriate and safe' and encouraged a 'consistent, evidence-based development' of CIM (Norgrove, 2011: para 4.106), the government's response merely set out its intentions regarding a 'child-centred approach' to family justice. It failed to address how the voice of the child would get heard or, indeed, how a child's best interests would be safeguarded when matters were agreed between parents out of court about their future:

> We agree with the Family Justice Review's view that a child's needs must always come first. We have to make it easier to make quicker decisions about a child's future care, and we have to make it easier for parents to settle their disagreements without going to court. Put simply, we want to make sure that the Family Justice System works best for children. This means changing things so that children's voices are heard at court, and they feel involved in decisions that affect them. Courts should ask children what they want and explain to them what is happening and why. (MoJ and DfE, 2012b: 3)

While this approach contained explicit and robust encouragement to parents to settle child arrangements without going to court, there was no indication that the child's views on arrangements agreed in mediation were needed, in contrast to the situation if the matter went to court. Indeed, while supporting the *Family Justice Review*'s view that mediation regarding children disputes must be 'child-centred', the government chose to substantially increase the public funding available for family mediation to provide *parents* with 'wider information and support'. The government concluded that 'for many couples, this level of support will be enough to help them agree on future arrangements for their children' (MoJ and DfE, 2012a: 21). There was no acknowledgement that young people might need or deserve information and support of their own, or that they should have a voice when future arrangements for them were being discussed and agreed.

Moreover, the response goes on to make an important assumption that continued parental involvement is likely to be the best course and that help is available to parents to achieve this, stating: 'When parents split up it is usually best for both parents to stay involved in caring for their children. We want to make sure that parents get help to agree how they can both give their children what is best for them – now and in the future' (MoJ and DfE, 2012b: 4).[1] The omission to consider the importance of a voice for children in post-separation arrangements affecting them stands out. Policy assumptions were made about what was best for children in general, but failed to consider how children might feel about any agreement reached. This shows that as a matter of policy, children are still regarded as legal objects rather than legal subjects, despite deep criticism of this approach made as long ago as 1988 in the Cleveland Report, which went on to call for children to be treated as 'people' not as 'objects of concern' (Butler-Sloss, 1988). This is even more concerning in the context of the UK having ratified the United Nations Convention on the Rights of the Child (UNCRC) in 1991, which gives explicitly to children capable of forming their own opinions the right to freely express a view on matters affecting their lives as appropriate to their age and understanding (article 12 UNCRC). Few things, we would suggest, directly affect a child's life more than a transition to new post-separation living arrangements following parental relationship breakdown. Children's article 12 rights have, at least in theory, been preserved within the court context (*Family Procedure Rules,*

---

[1] See also MoJ and DfE (2012a: 18).

Practice Direction 12B (PD12B: 4.4)). Here, the child's welfare is the court's paramount consideration (Children Act 1989 (CA 1989) s 1) with their wishes and feelings listed explicitly as a factor to consider (s 1(3)). However, in family mediation, while there is an expectation that children should be involved in the decision-making (PD12B: 4.4), there was and is no legal requirement to include children's views within the process, leaving their views and best interests in the hands of often conflicting parental narratives.

The principal idea for this book is, therefore, to add a critical dimension to the recent debates about family justice in general (Maclean and Eekelaar, 2016; Barlow, 2017; Hunter, 2017; Kaganas, 2017; Mant, 2022) and CIM in particular, by exploring some of these issues from the perspective of children themselves. While relationship breakdown has always been treated as a private and exclusively adult matter (Murch, 2018: 47), we question whether extending this thinking into making post-separation arrangements for children is the right approach, especially given the requirements of UNCRC article 12.

The impact of the neoliberal reforms

The significance of this lack of consideration of children's views in the out-of-court space grew when family mediation became the default process for resolving private family law disputes for those requiring legal aid. For this group, mediation was the only formal help available to parents after legally aided advice and representation were removed for most in April 2013. This policy was a central plank in efforts to 'encourage' take-up of family mediation and was delivered through the Legal Aid, Sentencing and Punishment of Offenders Act 2012 (LASPO). The *Family Justice Review* had not recommended the reform and envisaged legal advice remaining available. The Act withdrew legal aid for legal advice and representation in nearly all private family law disputes, including child arrangements, save in cases where objective proof of domestic violence was shown (Schedule 1, para 12(1) LASPO). It seemed to be primarily driven by cost-saving imperatives where one mediator for both parties was less expensive to the legal aid budget than access to a solicitor for each. It also hoped that offering mediation at an early stage would reduce the conflict between parents, encourage agreement and lead to fewer cases reaching the courts. In fact, the opposite was achieved with legally aided Mediation and Information Assessment Meetings down 60 per cent in 2020–1 compared with 2011–12; legally aided mediation starts halving over the same period, while private law children cases issued at court increased. These reached an all-time high in 2019 and have remained high since (JUSTICE, 2022: paras 2.10–2.12). However, 'empowering' separating couples to reach their own decisions, aided only by a mediator where needed, also fitted well with the concept of 'neoliberalism', a political philosophy embraced by the government of the day, which promoted an ethos of individualism and personal responsibility (Brown, 2006: 694; Stewart, 2007: 28; Barlow et al, 2017b: 2).

The practical outcome was that after the LASPO legal aid changes, most parents had to agree arrangements between themselves or through mediation, unless they were prepared to represent themselves in court or could afford to pay for legal advice and representation. It was a move which trumpeted the virtues of individualism and autonomy and denigrated the 'unnecessary' role of lawyers, financed by the state, in family disputes (Kaganas, 2017). Crucially, this approach left most children without any formal route to voice their views when arrangements were being made affecting them after parental separation, but out of court.

As we have argued elsewhere (Barlow et al, 2017b), the concepts of 'autonomy', 'responsibility' and 'neoliberalism' have driven current family justice reform and continue to influence policy and practice development around non-court family dispute resolution processes. They have each shaped current family mediation policy and practice but, to date, have led to parental concerns and financial constraints overshadowing any formal role for children being developed within non-court processes. Let us now reflect on how these conceptual drivers, which underpin family justice policy, assist or inhibit children's voices.

Theoretical framing and key concepts: neoliberal 'autonomy' and 'responsibility'

'Autonomy' is a cornerstone of neoliberal thinking, which, echoing the principles of the market, requires people to assume responsibility for 'navigating the social realm using rational choice' (Brown, 2006: 694). It is this forced 'responsibilization' (Reece, 2003), requiring a joint assumption of responsibility within the family mediation process but explained as (individual) autonomy, which is potentially problematic for all family dispute resolution and may act to exclude child consultation. Family mediation is premised upon the importance of private ordering, where the autonomy of the separating parties to voluntarily reach an agreement acceptable to them both about the arrangements for their children is key. As Roberts and Moscati (2020: 1) note, mediation's 'core values embody an ethic of respect – in particular, for the parties' own decision-making authority'. This can be seen in the emphasis within the Code of Practice on the process aiming to assist participants to 'reach decisions they consider appropriate to their own particular circumstances' (Family Mediation Council (FMC), 2018: 2.1). Indeed, Roberts (2014: 3) argues that it is this locating of decision-making authority with the parties and respect for party autonomy that distinguishes family mediation from other types of dispute resolution or professional interventions. Yet, there is often a clear tension between the autonomy of the parents involved. Each parent is likely to wish ideally for different outcomes to the other, or there would be no need for mediation. However, at present, within this area of family justice, autonomy is an adult-only concept, where most mediation is child-focused rather than child-inclusive (Barlow et al, 2017b). Thus, although the wishes and feelings of their child or children may pull in a different direction to one or both parents, there is no formal requirement to ascertain or consider these where parents agree.

Neoliberal 'autonomy' has already been exposed by Fineman (2004; 2013) and others (for example, Wallbank and Herring, 2014) as a myth, particularly in assumptions about capacity for both family and family law decision-making when factors other than one's individual free will based on rational thinking pull in different directions and affect 'choices'. In the family context, autonomy is, at best, 'relational' and is always subject to power dynamics, which can undermine 'rational' choice. The vulnerability of all the parties during the trauma of relationship breakdown, particularly in high-conflict disputes relating to children, is not an area where rational thinking and choices can safely prevail. The pursuit of agreements stressing party 'autonomy' and pushing 'responsibilization' is, therefore, potentially a high-risk strategy in family mediations involving high-conflict cases, where mediators must facilitate rather than advise. It is high risk not only because the chances of success are lower and power dynamics may be skewed, but also because there is the danger that separating-parent autonomy will be exercised to reach an agreement which is at odds not only with the wishes of the children themselves, but also with what family law would expect in terms of serving the best interests of children (Eekelaar and Maclean, 2013). As Diduck (2014: 618) has noted, decisions made by individuals in family disputes operate within a public and social context with public and social consequences. The removal by Children and Families Act 2014 ('the 2014 Act') section 17 of the previous requirement in the divorce context (Matrimonial Causes Act 1973, s 41) for courts to certify that the arrangements for children were satisfactory further illustrates the endorsement of parental autonomy and a wilful ignoring of what this might mean for children. Murch (2018: 156) points to the 'social paradox' of repealing the section 41 requirement to scrutinize arrangements for children, coupled with the failure to give children a voice within the Mediation and Information Assessment Meetings procedure introduced by the 2014 Act, at a time of growing and compelling national and international research highlighting the emotional fallout for children when parents separate.

Within the book, we will reflect on how well the emphasis on parental autonomy within child arrangement disputes is serving children, as well as consider the experiences of young people who participated in CIM and the outcomes of participation. Our analysis considers the mental health and wellbeing benefits to children when parents are brave enough to begin to cede that authority to their children so that they may participate meaningfully in the decision-making, in line with their evolving capacities, following parental separation. Taken together with our discussion of the requirements of article 12 UNCRC, we will call for a recasting of how the concept of 'autonomy' is constructed and understood within mediation of child arrangement disputes.

While Fineman (2013: 13) has noted the universality of vulnerability as part of the human condition and argues that legal responses should acknowledge this rather than assume autonomy is the appropriate driver, it is clear that children are the most vulnerable within family disputes. Indeed, their vulnerability may be magnified by their lack of agency. Private ordering is an attractive concept to many, but revisioning what autonomy or relational autonomy means in this context to give children themselves appropriate agency is an area we will explore further. In particular, we suggest that a concept of 'relational family autonomy' rather than just 'parental autonomy' should underpin family mediation practice and wider parental agreements about children on separation. Child arrangements are about children's lives post-separation and should involve the views and voices of all family members where appropriate, in order that a well-rounded discussion truly focused on children's best interests is achieved. Recognizing that children could and should have age-appropriate agency to participate in post-separation child arrangement planning at the point of parental separation and going forward, would help parents acknowledge that purely bilateral separated parent decision-making is not sufficiently relational, as it ignores the wishes, feelings and growing agency of their children. Understanding the importance of this as well as the international recognition of the right children have to play a role, would be a step towards achieving a shift to recognizing children as subjects or development actors, helping to frame their own best interests, rather than just objects of concern or passive beneficiaries whose interests are served in an adult-constructed decision-making process based on parental not family autonomy. In suggesting this, our analysis draws on notions within the UNCRC itself, which in articles 5 and 12 recognizes both the need for parents to guide children appropriately towards achieving full autonomy and agency, alongside a child's right to express views and have them taken seriously in matters affecting their lives. A relational approach to children's rights acknowledges that when children make choices (or choices are made for them) that take account of the interests of the wider family, this does not necessarily render the choice or decision non-autonomous, provided the family context is positive for the child and not oppressive. It further recognizes that children may need adult support to make decisions, but this does not render the decision non-autonomous (Hollingsworth and Stalford, 2017: 74–5). Embedding a 'relational family approach' into mediation practice, as we suggest, would keep the focus on finding workable solutions that meet the needs (and wishes) of the children primarily, as well as the wider family. As our earlier research has shown, invoking (parental) rights (Barlow et al, 2017b: 177) or, indeed, 'best interests' as a mask for parental rights (Smithson et al, 2015: 1) can set parents in opposition to each other, exacerbating conflict and making the mediation process less likely to succeed. A relational approach 'provides a rich resource for those seeking a more child-appropriate understanding of rights' (Hollingsworth and Stalford, 2017: 74). Above individual rights and freedoms, a relational approach seeks to promote values which support and uphold relationships (Herring, 2017: 262). It is an apposite approach since it aligns closely with a central aim of mediation – to facilitate separating parents to bring their relationship to an end in a way that 'promotes as good a relationship between [them] and their children as possible' (FMC, 2018: para 2.3b).

We therefore suggest here that within mediation of post-separation child arrangements, that autonomy, that is, the freedom to reach an agreement or joint decision, should be understood not purely as 'relational *parental* autonomy' where the parents are seen as the only active stakeholders in the process of reaching agreement, but as 'relational *family* autonomy', where the relationality within the process is actively extended to directly include and take seriously the children's perspectives.

Fineman (2013; 2019) calls for a responsive state that can reorient its policies to address needs arising from our universal vulnerability where appropriate. Given the inherent fallacies within the current neoliberal approach to parental autonomy, we feel it is vital to reflect on the family justice processes from children's perspectives, particularly given the UK's international obligations to consult children, and consider whether and how this may provide the impetus for reform.

Article 12 UNCRC: family justice for children

To consider the evidence on how well family law and the family justice system are combining to safeguard children and facilitate their voices in non-court processes within the reformed family justice landscape, we will use the UNCRC generally, and article 12 in particular, as a lens.

The UNCRC was drafted in 1989, the same year the CA 1989 was passed in England and Wales. The UK ratified it in 1991, just after the 1989 Act came into force, and it is now the most widely ratified human rights treaty, with 196 signatories.

It extends to everyone under 18 and aims not only to protect children worldwide but also to give them rights. This was a radical departure from the traditional view, where childhood was conceived merely as a journey towards adulthood, 'a process in which the boundary of becoming and being is crossed' (Lee, 2001: 8). As a result, children were categorized as dependent and passive, under the control of adults until the cliff edge moment when they reached the age of majority. Chronological age, Lee argues, can be a convenient 'mask of invisibility' which effectively conceals the shortcomings of some adults. He continues, '[t]he more one is in a position to make decisions for children, to speak on their behalf, the more one is able to silence their voices' (Lee, 2001: 10). In the context of family mediation, where adult parental narratives most often provide the only route to hearing children's voices, this is a pertinent observation.

Much has been written about the tension in the UNCRC between the need to protect children and the desire to give them rights appropriate to their age and maturity. Within academic literature, this is sometimes characterized as the 'rights v welfare' debate (Herring, 1999; Freeman, 2010). The juxtaposition of articles 3 and 12 of the UNCRC illustrates how children are at first wholly vulnerable and in need of protection but develop into young people with views who merit more agency.

Article 3(1) focuses on promoting and protecting their welfare or best interests: 'In all actions concerning children, whether undertaken by public or private social welfare institutions, courts of law, administrative authorities or legislative bodies, the best interests of the child shall be a primary consideration.' The wording of article 12, though, makes clear that children should have a say in the direction of their lives: 'States Parties shall assure to the child who is capable of forming his or her own views the right to express those views freely in all matters affecting the child, the views of the child being given due weight in accordance with the age and maturity of the child.'

Freeman (2010) explains that he does not see this as a tension or dichotomy. Rather, the UNCRC reflects a paradigm shift in how children are viewed, recognizing the complexity of their evolving status. Article 3 acknowledges children as 'becomings' by upholding their best interests. However, article 12 also recognizes them as 'beings' by giving them a voice.

Within the court context in England and Wales, the CA 1989 places the child's welfare as the paramount consideration in any court proceedings related to their upbringing (s 1(1)). In private law, this would encompass applications for child arrangements orders under section 8, which decide with whom a child should live and with whom they should have contact. Some acknowledgement of children's agency is contained in the section 1(3) welfare checklist, which places children's wishes and feelings at the top of a list of criteria the court must consider, without giving this factor any priority over other considerations. With leave of the court, a child can bring or be joined as a party to section 8 proceedings, providing the court is satisfied that they have 'sufficient understanding' to make the application (s 10(8)). These provisions are a part of the statutory enactment of the *Gillick* principle, according to which a child's agency increases (and parental rights/responsibility diminish) as they mature so that their capacity to make decisions should be increasingly respected, but may be context-specific, rather than universally achieved (*Gillick* v *W Norfolk and Wisbech Area Health Authority* [1986] AC 112).

However, there is a gap between the theory and practice even in the court space, with the 1989 Act not extending to non-court processes. Here, promoting the child's welfare in mediation or solicitor negotiation becomes a matter of professional conduct and is not enforceable in law as such (Family Law Protocol, 2010: para 1.5.1; see also FMC, 2018: para 5.7.1). Whether children are consulted in mediation was originally not even a matter which had to be raised with parents by the mediator at the initial Mediation and Information Assessment Meeting. However, following the *Final Report of the Voice of the Child*

Dispute Resolution Advisory Group (MoJ, 2015), the FMC, which sets standards for mediation nationally, amended its 'Standards Framework' in 2018 to require all mediators to attend CIM awareness or update training and explain CIM to prospective clients. However, it can only proceed if both parents consent *and* the mediator is suitably qualified to conduct CIM. For children capable of forming their own views, even though article 12(2) adds the caveat that a child may be heard 'either directly, or through a representative or an appropriate body in a manner consistent with the procedural rules of national law', this parental gatekeeping approach hardly seems in line with the text of article 12(1).

Children's rights and 'evolving capacities': space, voice, audience and influence

How compatible is this parental gatekeeping approach with the requirements of the UNCRC, given the provisions of article 12? The answer may differ for children of different ages and maturity, and the Convention recognizes that parents have responsibilities, rights and duties regarding their children. Article 5 refers to children's 'evolving capacities' and recognizes a balance needs to be struck: 'State Parties shall respect the responsibilities, rights and duties of parents ... to provide, in a manner consistent with the evolving capacities of the child, appropriate direction and guidance in the exercise by the child of the rights recognized in the present Convention.'

The relationship between articles 5 and 12 is recognized as having 'special relevance' (UNCRC General Comment No. 12, 2009: para 69). Children's participation may stimulate the development of the child's evolving capacities (UNCRC General Comment No. 12, 2009: para 79). Equally, as the child's capacity evolves, the parent's responsibilities transform from 'direction and guidance into reminders and advice and later to an exchange on an equal footing' (UNCRC General Comment No. 12, 2009: para 84). This chimes with the nuanced approach developed in domestic law through the *Gillick* principle. As Lansdown (2005: 3) argues, the concept of 'evolving capacities' embodies the balance in the Convention between 'recognising children as active agents in their own lives, entitled to be listened to, respected and granted increasing autonomy in the exercise of rights, while also being entitled to protection in accordance with their relative immaturity and youth'. Yet, even considering article 5 and the article 12(2) caveat noted earlier, the parental veto to child consultation within the current family mediation process approach still seems to challenge the requirements of article 12(1).

To explore whether adopting the UNCRC into domestic law might assist children in the non-court family dispute resolution context, we will also draw on Tobin's (2015) critique of Fineman's 'vulnerability theory'. Echoing Freeman (2010), this argues that the UNCRC is predicated on rights, in which children's vulnerability is recognized but is balanced against their evolving capacities and participatory rights so that they are not only seen but heard and listened to. We will use this to assess whether CIM could provide a stepping stone towards achieving a similar balance in the out-of-court space, but this will require the state to respond actively.

As we have suggested elsewhere (Barlow et al, 2024), given the gap between the theory and practice of hearing children's voices even where matters do reach court, and the lack of facilitation of direct consultation with children out of court, it seems likely that in England, where the UNCRC has not been incorporated into domestic law, there may well be non-compliance with the requirements of the Convention and particularly article 12, which does explicitly extend to mediation (UNCRC General Comment No. 12, 2009: para 32). Indeed, this view is endorsed by concern recently expressed by the UN Committee on the Rights of the Child itself as part of its monitoring process about a lack of respect for children's views. In its concluding observations of the sixth and seventh periodic reports of the UK, it notes that children's views are not systematically considered in decisions affecting them and underscores the importance of the availability of age-appropriate information to facilitate child participation (UNCRC Committee, 2023: para 23). It goes on to recommend that the UK government should take action to '[e]nsure the right of all children … to express their views and to have them taken into account in all decisions affecting them, including in courts and relevant judicial proceedings and regarding domestic violence, custody … education, justice, migration and asylum' (UNCRC Committee, 2023: para 23(a)). It further called upon the government to '[s]trengthen measures to promote the *meaningful participation* of children in family, community and school settings and in policymaking at the local and national levels' (UNCRC Committee, 2023: para 23(b), emphasis added).

Incorporation of the UNCRC may provide a good way forward for realizing children's rights in the family law context. However, there needs to be more clarity around precisely what incorporation of article 12 into domestic law might mean and how it might operate in a way that respects the concept of children's evolving capacities, which is fundamental to understanding children's rights (Varadan, 2019).

To further inform the debate, Lundy (2007: 930) has argued that article 12 is 'one of the most widely cited yet commonly misunderstood of all of the provisions of the UNCRC'. She contends that common abbreviations, including 'the voice of the child', 'the right to be heard', 'the right to participate' and/ or 'the right to be consulted', though useful shorthand, dilute the impact of article 12 and imperfectly reflect its contents. Instead, she advocates a four-stage test to ensure compliance with article 12. There must be 'space' (children must be given the opportunity to express a view); 'voice' (children must be facilitated to express their views); 'audience' (the child's view must be listened to); and 'influence' (the child's view must be acted upon, as appropriate) (Lundy, 2007: 933). We will consider the psychological benefits to young people of having 'space', 'voice', 'audience' and 'influence' from the perspectives of relationship professionals and the young people themselves in Chapter Two. We reflect on how the first three stages were accommodated in young people's experiences of CIM in Chapter Four, reflecting simultaneously on how their evolving capacities must be acknowledged and accommodated in article 12 compliant services. In Chapter Five, we explore the issue of whether the child's views influenced outcomes.

Clearly, the age and understanding of the child is important as to whether they are seen only as vulnerable and in need of protection, or a 'being' with rights, capable of some agency in the decision-making at hand. Freeman (2010: 16) argues that rights are critical because 'they recognize the respect the bearers are owed. To accord rights is to respect dignity'. Furthermore, 'those who have them can exercise agency' and, in turn, agents can participate and make decisions (Freeman, 2010: 17). Freeman's view at the time of writing was that it was necessary to fight for the recognition of children's rights despite Westminster being 'at best equivocal' about children's rights (Freeman, 2010: 27). He noted that the Equality Act 2010 does not include children and the Children's Rights Bill, which would have incorporated the UNCRC into English law, was moved in the House of Lords on 19 November 2009 but made no further progress. Yet, given that the reporting mechanisms under the Convention have not succeeded in prompting action, he concludes that the case for incorporating the UNCRC is 'convincing' (Freeman, 2010: 27). How far the legal and political landscapes have moved to make this more realizable remains to be seen. However, our research has revealed young people's strong desire for their views on parental separation to be taken more seriously.

Young people and child-inclusive mediation: research, methods and practice

As explained more fully in Appendix I, the *Healthy Relationship Transitions (HeaRT)* study was part of a wider two-year interdisciplinary project, funded by the Wellcome Centre for the

Cultures and Environments of Health, *Transforming Relationships and Relationship Transitions with and for the Next Generation.* Overall, this aimed to understand the potential role of relationship education in facilitating young people's agency and access to support about relationships, including parental separation. It also examined the experiences of children and their parents who had participated in CIM, alongside the views of relationship professionals (mostly counsellors) working with separated families and family mediators regarding its value and drawbacks.

The idea for *HeaRT* came from research findings in our earlier national study of non-court processes, which identified a concerning lack of both CIM uptake and UK research into children's views on how they would view the opportunity to participate (Ewing et al, 2015; Barlow et al, 2017b: 210). While the earlier study, *Mapping Paths to Family Justice* (*Mapping*), was not designed to seek out children's views, it did establish that there were high numbers of family mediators nationally accredited to conduct child consultation as part of the mediation process but low take-up of it. The reasons given by practitioners and parents for not pursuing CIM were a combination of a lack of confidence on the part of the mediators about their capacity to do this well, and parental refusal to allow children to participate, wanting to protect their children from the dispute as much as possible (Barlow et al, 2017b).

As noted, since this study, the FMC has amended its Standards Framework in 2018 to include more CIM awareness and update training. CIM has also been suggested as a process that could significantly improve outcomes for children whose parents are separating (Family Solutions Group, 2020; JUSTICE, 2022). The *HeaRT* study itself therefore set out to explore how CIM practice had developed since the *Mapping* research and what the views of wider relationship experts as well as family mediators were on the calls for expansion of CIM, alongside the views and experiences of parents and in particular, young people themselves, about which there was little or no evidence.

Our research design, rationale and methods are set out fully in Appendix I. It is important to note that the names of all participants have been anonymized. Any names referred to in this book are pseudonyms, with adults ascribed surnames to distinguish them from young people.

In summary here, a qualitative and engaged approach to this empirical study was adopted. This involved interactive panel sessions with a range of young people at the beginning and then the end of the study to co-create its aims and findings; a reflexive workshop with 11 CIM mediators and three family justice professionals to understand the CIM process and models of good and bad practice; ten semi-structured telephone interviews with wider relationship professionals to gain their insight into the benefits and drawbacks of CIM; 20 qualitative semi-structured interviews with a sample of CIM qualified family mediators; four focus groups with a total of 18 diverse Family Justice Young People's Board members aged 11–19 who had experienced parental separation to gather their views on the risks and benefits of CIM as well as young people's information and support needs. An interview was also conducted with a young adult family law campaigner using the same focus group schedule as used for the focus groups on information and support needs. We used semi-structured interviews with our participants who had directly experienced CIM, comprising 20 young people (nine girls and 11 boys, aged 9–19) and 12 parents (five fathers and seven mothers).

Against the background of calls for wider inclusion of children's voices in family mediation and concerns about the UK's UNCRC compliance, we will consider the implications of the findings from the *HeaRT* study (Barlow et al, 2022) for a children's rights agenda.

What child-inclusive mediation offers

Given that family mediation remains the central means through which family disputes involving children are encouraged to be resolved and given the current crisis within the family courts, which are overburdened (Law Society, 2023), might finding a truly child-centred way of including children's views help reset family justice on a new and improved path? Murch (2018: 255) calls for a radical reimagining of the family justice system. He argues that it should retain its constitutional independence but become more hybrid; part of the community's preventive mental health services. Its aim should be to promote children's emotional resilience and wellbeing within the context of helping parents recover from the emotional turbulence associated with relationship breakdown. This book will explore the role that CIM, re-envisioned through a children's rights lens, might play in promoting children's emotional resilience and wellbeing when parents separate.

While mediation did not traditionally include child consultation, this practice has gained ground as a useful mediation tool over time. Research has already revealed some advantages of consulting children when parents separate. They tend to be more satisfied with the arrangements (Butler et al, 2002: 96; Parkinson and Cashmore, 2008: 75). Arrangements also tend to be longer lasting, with father–child relationships benefiting. In addition, it often results in a style of post-separation parenting which is more cooperative (Walker and Lake-Carroll, 2014: 40). In two studies, one in Australia (McIntosh et al, 2008) and one in England and Wales, interviewing adults whose parents had separated when they were children (Fortin et al, 2012), consulting young people on child arrangements had been found to have the potential to ameliorate the adverse effects of parental separation for children and their parents by reducing parental conflict. However, only limited legal aid funding was made available for the practice of CIM following the LASPO reforms. In addition, as Parkinson (2020) documents, there are different models of CIM, but all involve the mediator consulting the child separately from the parents. While CIM dates back to the 1980s in England and Wales, it was initially only practised by relatively few mediators, mostly from a therapeutic background (Parkinson, 2020). Despite the Council of Europe's recommendation in 2003 that children should be heard in mediation (Council of Europe Recommendation, 2003: 4), it remained a 'minority activity' (Walker and Lake-Carroll, 2014: 41). While the 2016 version of the FMC's Code of Practice required that '*[a]ll* children and young people aged 10 and above should be offered the opportunity to have their voices heard directly during the Mediation, if they wish' (FMC, 2016: 5.7.2, emphasis added), it was not until 2018, following the recommendations of the FMC's 2017 CIM Working Group introducing compulsory update training for CIM-trained mediators and awareness training for all other family mediators, that renewed focus on the practice enhanced the potential for greater uptake. Perhaps because of this renewed focus, FMC surveys revealed an increase in cases in which children aged ten and over were consulted – 26 per cent in 2019 (FMC, 2019), up from 14 per cent in the 2017 survey (FMC, 2017). However, the response rate to the 2019 survey was only 12 per cent of FMC members. Additionally, there is no requirement to keep records of the number of children seen, so there is no definitive picture of how many children get to exercise their right to be heard in mediation, should they so wish, but this is estimated to be around 3,200 children per annum (Family Solutions Group, 2020: 105). While this is likely to be far more than are given 'space' and a 'voice' in other out-of-court processes, such as solicitor negotiations and collaborative law, for which no data is available (JUSTICE, 2022: para 2.47), but which have no established means of eliciting children's views, more can and should be done in mediation to blaze a trail towards greater child-inclusive practice.

What children think about CIM has not, until now, been explored. This book addresses that gap in the knowledge base, drawing on empirical findings from the *HeaRT* study, which aimed to understand CIM from all perspectives, including those of children, parents, mediators and relationship professionals.

Chapter Two focuses on the views of the relationship professionals (and young people) on the psychological, wellbeing and agency benefits (and risks) of giving children a voice in the decision-making when parents separate, particularly in CIM. The barriers to uptake of CIM are examined in Chapter Three, while Chapter Four considers the experiences of the process from the point of view of the children and their parents. Chapter Five examines which families were able to resolve matters in CIM and whether the children and parents were satisfied with the outcomes.

Finally, in Chapter Six, we draw together our conclusions. We consider, based on our evidence, the changes needed to realize a mediation system which is fully compliant with article 12 UNCRC, and the role of a UK children's rights framework to redress the current norm of children being heard by proxy through parental narratives, allowing parental autonomy to side-step the need to truly listen to children's voices, as children transform from 'becoming' to 'being' over time.

Using our findings alongside other research, ultimately, in this book, we answer the question posed of whether the time has come for children to be considered 'subjects' rather than 'objects' of the family justice system in England and Wales.

TWO

Children's Right to Be Heard?
Points of View from Relationship
Professionals and Children

Introduction

As we saw in Chapter One, aside from fulfilling children's international rights to information and consultation, other research (McIntosh et al, 2008; Fortin et al, 2012) has shown that consulting children about arrangements when parents separate brings mental health and wellbeing benefits to young people. Yet, such a process may also contain risks or may not be something children themselves want. This chapter now focuses on the interviews with relationship professionals working with or for separated parents and their children outside of the mediation context, outlining whether, *in principle*, they believed that young people ought to be given a voice in the decision-making when parents separate and the psychological, wellbeing and agency benefits (and risks) of doing so. It also explores their views on child-inclusive mediation (CIM)'s role in giving young people a voice. Its analysis compares these views with those of young people in focus groups on these questions. Unless otherwise indicated, the findings in this chapter from young people are the focus group participants' views. However, where young people who engaged in CIM comment on the *principle* of giving young people a voice, these are also discussed, with their experiences of the process and outcomes *in practice* discussed in Chapters Four and Five, respectively.

Embedding the concept of 'relational family autonomy' in CIM, and indeed in family justice more broadly, will require an acceptance, *in principle*, that children have a right to be heard and their views given due weight in the decision-making when parents separate, per their evolving capacities. Indeed, as we demonstrate in Chapter Three, unless the two critical gatekeepers to CIM – the mediators and the parents – grasp the benefits of giving young people a voice *in principle*, they will likely find it difficult to overcome obstacles to make engaging in CIM a reality.

The mental health and wellbeing benefits to young people of recognizing them as subjects and not merely objects of decision-making that the relationship professionals and young people raise should provide impetus for the conceptual, statutory and procedural changes needed to realize the article 12 compliant system we envision as outlined in Chapter Six.

Hearing from young people: the views of the relationship professionals

The relationship professionals were unanimous – young people need an outlet to process their feelings following parental separation. There was less agreement on whether CIM should be the preferred forum, with three professionals expressing reservations about the process or considering that children's needs are better met in, or alongside, counselling. Almost all thought that young people should have a voice in the decision-making process and spoke of the health and wellbeing benefits this brings. There was also strong support for a more holistic child-centred response to parental separation than at present.

An outlet

The relationship professionals were unanimous that young people need an outlet to process their feelings when parents separate. However, three out of ten expressed reservations about CIM as this outlet. Clara Farley questioned whether mediators have the requisite skills to deal with older children's complex emotions: "I am very dubious [of CIM] … mediation comes at the wrong time for the wrong people in the wrong way." She doubted mediators had the requisite training "to manage the complexity of the emotional discharge that is going on". Clara praised the quality of advice that young people received from neutral third parties at ChildLine, helping them to make sense of their place in the family post-separation. She felt that while mediation has its place, CIM or counselling can be counterproductive when the parents are still locked in high conflict. Clara preferred a family therapy-based model over CIM as the former "create[s] safety for conversations that are painful and difficult". She thought the offer should be universal, easily accessible, community-based and made at a time and in a format (including remotely) that meets the needs of individual children.

Fran Clarkson thought children need a "neutral space" in which to process their feelings and that a discrete therapeutic intervention that is "just for the child" is preferable to CIM because the latter "implies that the child is being included in … what the parents are doing". She expressed concern that CIM might unnecessarily burden the child. She favoured an early triage of the child's needs and a referral accordingly. This might be into CIM, but would more likely be to child or family therapy, sometimes alongside CIM.

Rosemary Allen took a somewhat paternalistic stance: "The adults are the judges; the adults make the final decision." She conceded that CIM has a role, but only to explain the decisions that the parents have reached. In Rosemary's view, counselling could provide the outlet children need to think through, express and have validated their feelings on these significant changes in their lives. However, while highlighting that children must not be burdened with making choices, and the need for mediators to have the requisite skills, most relationship professionals said that hearing from children *during* the mediation process and allowing children's views to inform the parents' decisions is psychologically beneficial to children. Acknowledging the psychological benefits of giving young people 'space', 'voice', 'audience' and 'influence' (Lundy, 2007: 933), Shelly Jennings summed up the majority view:

'It is so powerful in so many ways for a young person to be heard and to be given a situation where they can ... say how they feel and pass those opinions via someone else to their parents. ... It is not about giving the full power and control to the child or young person to say, "whatever you decide, is going to be what will happen", but it is about being heard.'

Giving young people "a situation" (space) "where they can ... say how they feel and pass those opinions via someone else to their parents" (voice) in which they are "heard" (audience) and what they say is taken into account even if they are not given "full power and control ... [to] decide" (influence) is powerful, in the view of most of the relationship professionals.

Fleur Dowson thought that it was essential to give young people a forum in which to "offload" and that it was vital for professionals to listen, as you can gain more from the young person's account than the parent's, as the parent "might not be attached to the child or in tune with them". Jacob Beardsley thought that it is "always worthwhile talking to children", but he lamented the fact that despite there being "a whole world of talk" about the need to listen to children and young adults, "we all seem to struggle with the idea that *actually* we are going to talk to them". He also thought that inroads into hearing from children systematically when parents separate are unlikely until there is an acknowledgement of just how difficult it is for parents, already in a state of emotional turmoil, to be open to the terrifying prospect that in giving their child any element of choice, the child might choose against them. Parents often reject an offer to involve their children for fear of what they might say (Cashmore and Parkinson, 2008: 96).

Voice not choice

Rosemary Allen said that when parents separate, children need sensitive explanations about and support to adjust to decisions made by their parents but should not be consulted about the decision. She acknowledged that mediators could help parents consider whether decisions are judicious and have accounted for the child's needs and desires. However, she was adamant that:

'You don't consult with the child. It's not the child's choice ... You will tell the child what is going to happen, but you do not burden the child with what is not his or her choice, and when the choice is made, you explain it, and you understand what the child will be feeling [but] ... you do not go to the child for advice about what to do.'

The other relationship professionals supported hearing from children but distinguished this from allowing young people to be the decision-makers. Kay Eagles encapsulated this viewpoint. She strongly supported CIM and saw the skilled mediator's role as one of helping parents "to understand that it is absolutely not about the child being the decision-maker, making decisions, or indeed making choices, but it is about the fact that the child is an interested person in this, and it is their lives that are going to change forever and enormously".

Non-child-inclusive mediation interventions and support

Despite majority support for CIM, most relationship professionals favoured the opportunity and space for the child to process their feelings in a therapeutic environment. Several cautioned against using the term 'counselling' or 'therapy' in this context as it risks pathologizing the child rather than acknowledging the support needed through a challenging life phase.

The referral might be as an alternative to CIM or alongside the process. Some felt that counselling in a school setting could be helpful, and some that a discrete, independent offering outside the school environment might be best as schools have a relationship with the parents. Others considered that there is a place for peer forums to support young people, online and in person. If they are sufficiently neutral, grandparents can provide stability and support to children when parents separate.

The views of the young people

The views of the young people we spoke to reflect those consistently reported in this jurisdiction (Smart and Neale, 1999; Walker and Lake-Carroll, 2014; Barlow et al, 2017a) and internationally (Cashmore and Parkinson, 2008; Parkinson and Cashmore, 2008: 64; Bell et al, 2021) – they want a voice in the decision-making when parents separate. They desire 'a bigger voice more of the time' (Carson et al, 2018: 68).

A right

In the interviews and focus groups, young people were unanimous; passionately, they believed that children should have a right to be heard (if they so wish) when parents separate, and adults must facilitate that right, listen to and act upon children's views.

In the focus groups, Farah told us, "Just because I am a kid, it doesn't mean that my parents' decisions are the be-all and end-all; I do have a right. If I am uncomfortable or if I feel unsafe or whatever it is, I have a right to be heard." Grace felt that failing to consult young people "when it's their lives and their time that is changing" would be "really stupid", pointing out the obvious, namely that, "You don't know what [children] are actually thinking until they tell you."

Many young people interviewed echoed the focus group participants' frustration. Anna said that for young people, "not to be able to have a voice seems really crazy". Harry said that it would be "pretty selfish" to deny children their rights. Alfie's advice to parents considering the process was: "If you want what's best for your child, then let them have a go because it will release a lot of stress from their chest and make them a lot more of a happier person." Joel's advice to young people considering the process was that "having your opinion expressed is one of the most valuable things to do and can help things for the better for you".

None of the young people in interview spoke of United Nations Convention of the Rights of the Child (UNCRC) rights (a closely guarded adult secret), yet all instinctively believed that children should have the right to be heard. Jonny told us that young people "should have a right to ... make the decisions" as "it's their family too". Equally important was the parents' "duty" to listen to their children (Greg). While ignorant of their article 12 rights, instinctively, young people thought they ought to be given 'space', 'voice', 'audience' and 'influence' (Lundy, 2007: 933) in decision-making.

The Family Justice Young People's Board (FJYPB) comprises young people with 'direct experience of the family justice system or an interest in children's rights' (FJYPB website).[1] Consequently, it was unsurprising that among the focus group participants, advocacy for child-inclusive processes was often framed from a rights perspective and with a level of awareness around young people's rights in court proceedings that was, understandably, less evident in the interviews with young people who had experienced CIM. Craig, for example,

---

[1] See: https://www.cafcass.gov.uk/children-and-young-people/family-just ice-young-peoples-board

lamented the lack of an independent advocate for children in private law proceedings when, in public law proceedings, they would have that independent representation.

A given

With the caveat that mediators must have the requisite skills, young people thought hearing from children in mediation should be a given. Martin said, "If it gets the voice of the child out, why wouldn't you do it?" In interview, Harry thought that CIM should "definitely" be made available to children nationally because probably without it, "their voices would sort of be lost". This strong support among young people for mechanisms to facilitate hearing from them ('space' and 'voice') reflects consistent pleas from young people in research internationally, as mentioned earlier.

Voice and choice

Whereas the relationship professionals who supported hearing from children stressed that the adults remained the decision-makers, the young people were clear that not only should they have the right to be heard, but, in line with the children's autonomy principle (Daly, 2018a; 2018b), their views should be taken seriously and generally followed. Blake emphasized that parents should listen to what their children wanted, and if this did not coincide with the parents' preferences, the parents "should probably go with what the child might want as they will probably know what they want best".

Universal

In the focus groups (reflecting similar messages from the young people who had experienced CIM), participants thought there should be flexibility over the age at which young people are heard, recognizing that young people mature differently. Initially, Grace was judged too young to be heard in mediation. She was allowed to participate once it was realized "how headstrong and mature" she was and said that without mediation, she would have been left in a dangerous situation. Natasha said that considering the child's views should be the default. She was adamant that even very young children needed information. She had not understood what was happening until she was eight or nine and found it "really frustrating because you are not really told what's happening about your own life". The focus group participants aged 11 to 15 were unanimous that children as young as four or five should have an opportunity to be heard. Jimmy thought that younger children might be more honest with the mediator, whereas, understanding the situation better, older children might fear being open.

Reflecting the views of his peers, Max said that young people "should be involved as much as they can just because it's their life that's being decided about ... you should [not] ... let your parents decide ... what's going to happen in your life when it's not their life that they are making decisions for!"

In the older group (16 plus), Aleah thought that all children should be given the option of attending CIM because even if a young child talked about "random" things, the parents' approach would be "more child focused". She regretted not having been given the option of participating, reflecting that if this had been an option, "at least you could have said years later, well I was offered this at that stage, whether you took it ... it's nice to have known that that opportunity is there".

UNCRC article 5 recognizes children's right to parental guidance and direction to secure the enjoyment of their rights consistent with their evolving capacities (Tobin and Varadan, 2019). Furthermore, article 5 'recognises the child, irrespective of age, as an active participant in their own development, entitled to be afforded opportunities for the gradual acquisition of greater autonomy' (Lansdown, 2022: 122). Young people we spoke to saw it as the responsible adults' duty to think carefully about how children's views would be incorporated rather than them simply being "branded as too young to know [their] own opinion", as Farah put it, and as had been the experience of many.

This group was adamant that while CIM attendance should be voluntary, the child, not the parents, should be the arbiter. Otherwise, the children who most need to have their voices heard may be denied the chance – reflecting the concern of Freeman (2010: 22) on rights more generally. As Aleah put it:

'The children who should actually be listened to are the ones that won't get listened to ... because the parents will say, "No, I don't want you to mess with my child, no, no, no, they speak to me, they don't need to speak to strangers, you know, I want to keep them young".'

Participants in the younger group were similarly frustrated that young people do not get "to choose whether they are involved or not, even though it is their life!" (Natasha).

Non-child-inclusive mediation interventions and support

While the young people viewed CIM as an essential mechanism for facilitating children's voices, like the relationship professionals, they did not see it as the only outlet. The online FJYPB focus groups considered young people's information and support needs when parents separate. One group canvassed the possibility of a 'buddy system' in schools, since support need not come from adults only. Others suggested support from school pastoral teams and appropriate therapy or counselling. Now an adult, Louise said she had not appreciated how her parents' acrimonious divorce affected her confidence at work and trust in relationships. Her employer paid for counselling for her divorce trauma, which she had found beneficial. She reflected that having it earlier "would have saved me a lot of heartache".

Ultimately, the focus group members favoured a suite of support options, one of which would be CIM. Carefully monitored peer forums were suggested as part of a one-stop-shop website (see Chapter Three). A range of therapeutic, CIM or other support should be offered, with attendance optional and the decision to participate child-led. As Katie told us, "[You should] not be told you have to do something … [instead, you should be] given the options and then you can choose who you want to speak to, or you don't want to speak to, or what you want to do."

Consistent with international research (Carson et al, 2018: 94) and calls for skilled, empathetic support from key 'first responders' such as teachers (Murch, 2018: 201), focus group participants said schools should inform them of their rights and provide support when parents separate, as discussed further in Chapter Three.

The following sections outline the perceived risks and benefits of CIM, identified by both relationship professionals and young people.

The risks of child-inclusive mediation

Both groups were alive to the possible risks of CIM and emphasized the need for highly skilled mediators to conduct this work. Margot Hendon reflected the majority view: "I think it takes tremendous skill to create … an interaction with that [young] person [in] which … they feel that they have been listened to."

Pressure

The relationship professionals who expressed reservations about including young people in mediation feared it risked putting too much pressure on the child, drawing the children into the separation to an inappropriate extent. Fran Clarkson said that she "got" the arguments about giving children a voice so that they felt a part of the decision-making, but thought "perhaps that overburdens them, and that actually good parents deal with this and … don't put their children in difficult positions where they are worried about what they say". Fran feared parents could use CIM defensively, and Margot Hendon that they might subsequently cross-examine their child. In interviews and focus groups, the young people shared these reservations. They were adamant that participation must be the child's decision; the right must include a right *not* to be heard if they choose.

As Butler et al (2002: 98) argue, children *are* involved in their parents' separation and the emotional turmoil that often accompanies this, whether we allow them to be involved in the decision-making or not. The young people were pragmatic; parental separation can be traumatic, so voicing your opinions through a neutral third party, such as a mediator, might relieve some pressure. As Harry, in interview, told us, "[Whether] you are talking to your parents or a mediator, there is always going to be some level of pressure on you." Becky concluded that parental separation is "inevitably" hurtful for a child. Therefore, if we give them "a platform to be able to raise kind of how they are upset about it and being able to speak about what is bothering them about arrangements" ('space' and a 'voice'), "surely that's better than just leaving them to get on with what's decided" (thereby denying them their right to 'audience' and 'influence').

Layla felt that children could feel muddled and easily influenced by their parents' accounts. Talking to a mediator, who is not involved in the family, helps the young person to put the situation into perspective and lets parents hear the child's views "without the influence of either parent". Far from adding pressure, therefore, giving a child a voice could relieve pressure, particularly for young people whose relationship with at least one parent is problematic. Nevertheless, alive to the possible pressure that children could be placed under, especially if their views contradicted the views of one parent, they underscored the need for careful screening for suitability on a case-by-case basis. Both the professionals and young people emphasized the need for highly skilled mediators. They also highlighted young people's resilience. As Katie pointed out, "Children often are more resilient than we think they are … if they are already going through [parental separation], they have already got a level of resilience, and actually hearing about it might just help."

Manipulation

Allied with the concern that consulting the child may put them under pressure, the relationship professionals and young people highlighted the risk that a parent might manipulate a child. Anna highlighted that the child's views might be unreliable if a parent presses for child consultation to assist their case.

Parents not listening

As with feelings of pressure, when interviewed, Harry thought that with or without mediation, there was a risk that parents would not listen to or take the child's views seriously but that "at least with mediation, there is another adult who understands the child and [can] … convey their message to the parents". In his interview, Richard said they were more likely to listen to someone their age explaining the issue than a child.

Recognizing that parents may not want to hear their child's views, focus group participants underscored the need for parents to put the child at the centre of the decision-making. Becky advised that parents must "take on board" what the child is saying ('audience' and 'influence'), focusing on the child's long-term interests rather than beating the other parent. Layla thought that "a lot of parents have that 'I know my child best' mindset, and no one else can tell me … how my child is". She encouraged such parents to put their "pride aside" and "listen to the people who are trying to help you, and listen to your child".

The benefits of child-inclusive mediation

The relationship professionals and young people spoke of mental health and welfare benefits, such as feeling less anxious and more reassured, that flowed from upholding their right to be heard. Dimopoulos (2021: 440) suggests that young people have a right to 'decisional privacy', that is a right to participate actively and meaningfully in decision-making about matters that affect them while demonstrating respect for their evolving capacity for autonomy. As conceptualized by Dimopoulos, decisional privacy is relational, recognizing that children's rights and interests are intertwined with those of their parents and other family members (Dimopoulos, 2021: 442). This relational dimension is central to the 'relational family autonomy' concept we propose. Conceptualizing the approach this way should shift the current balance of autonomy between parents and young people when decisions are made out of court. The 'Lundy Model of Child Participation' then assists with how these conceptual changes may be operationalized. Facilitating the expression of young people's views ('space' and 'voice') and respecting their evolving capacity for autonomy ('audience' and 'influence'), our evidence shows, has mental health benefits for young people.

Informing the child

In the context of parental separation, the availability and accessibility of information for young people 'is the crucial starting point in any child rights-based approach to dispensing justice' (Stalford et al, 2017: 208). Research shows that, following parental separation, feelings of uncertainty and fear that decisions will be made without their involvement distresses children (Butler et al, 2002: 93; Barlow et al, 2017a: 20). The relationship professionals concurred that providing children with a mechanism for hearing their voices when parents separate informs them of what is happening, helping the child adjust to the separation. Lack of information can delay children's recovery. As Jacob Beardsley put it, "What stymies [children processing grief on separation] is not knowing what's going on ... so you can't identify the loss that you need to grieve, you can't put into language what it is that is happening." A secondary benefit was that hearing from young people could inform how the mediator works with the parents.

The focus group participants were adamant that when parents separate, young people need better information and support than is currently available. This information needed to be easily accessible, non-stigmatizing and tailored to the needs of individual children, particularly in cases featuring domestic abuse. It must be in a format and time that meets children's needs individually, recognizing that some children prefer lots of information upfront, whereas others "might just want to slowly absorb what's going on" (Becky). The information could come from various sources, particularly schools or via a trusted website. The focus group participants agreed, however, that CIM also had a place in providing young people with the information and support they needed at this emotionally challenging time in their lives. They suggested that when parents separate young people need information on the process (What needs to be sorted out? Who makes the decisions? How long will it take? What say would they have in decisions made?), the practicalities (What would change? What would stay the same?) and the support available, including how young people can access it.

Reflecting previous research (O'Quigley, 2000; Walker and Lake-Carroll, 2014; Barlow et al, 2017a; Carson et al, 2018), most said that they had not had sufficient information and that this had adversely affected their recovery from the parental separation. Jasmine, for example, disclosed that, unlike her younger sibling, she had had little information or support when her parents separated and had not known what was happening. Reflecting the relationship professionals' views, she felt that this harmed her in later years. She said, "The separation developed issues with me over the years ... even though it may not have affected me during that moment, over years to come, it did."

As will be seen in Chapter Four, the reported experiences of the young people confirmed what the relationship professionals believed to be the case; giving young people an outlet to help them process their grief and be better informed about the process can hugely benefit their psychological wellbeing and recovery. Having experienced CIM, Alfie thought the process would help other young people in his situation to bring "clarity to the kids".

Reassuring the child

Several relationship professionals said that providing young people with an outlet can reassure them that they are not to blame for the separation. Shelly Jennings thought that young people are "like sponges, and if you don't fill in the gaps ... they will make up their own minds as to what's going on ... and they will typically blame themselves". Fleur Dowson indicated that without a voice in the process, children often carry this sense of blame into adulthood, leading many to seek therapy at that stage.

Reflecting similar messages from the young people who experienced CIM, the focus group participants felt that giving young people a voice could provide valuable reassurance, particularly if coercive control or abuse is disclosed. Speaking to a neutral third party rather than a parent helps young people, in Layla's view, to put their feelings into perspective.

Respecting the child

According rights respects the dignity of the bearer (Freeman, 2010). Listening to children is a positive symbol of respect (Lansdown, 2001). Several relationship professionals recognized that young people value being included in decision-making and that hearing from children accords respect. As Kay Eagles put it, "Young people really, really value being included ... the most helpful thing you can do is just give [children] a forum in which they can talk ... and be heard ... children need to have a voice because it's their life." As explored in Chapter Three, some mediators and parents were prone to focusing on the progress towards a settlement that can be reached when a child is consulted. However, the relationship professionals focused on the mental health benefits to young people of valuing their input, regardless of whether this aided settlement. Hugo Greening told us, "If I give you a voice, it makes you feel valued. That's the key bit. It may not change things, but I have been heard." Hugo also felt that, particularly for children who are not yet developmentally able to articulate their feelings fully, having a space where their hurt and anger are acknowledged and normalized can be beneficial.

The young people agreed that hearing from young people accords them with respect and dignity, as Freeman (2010) suggests, and they urged parents to take up the option of CIM. As Becky argued, giving young people a "platform" such as CIM through which to explain their feelings is "surely ... better than just leaving them to get on with what's decided".

Improving family relationships

From the perspective of the relationship professionals who favoured CIM, one benefit is that it can help children and parents better understand the other's position, improving relationships within the family. As Kay Eagles explained, "the sort of 'we are all in it together' bit can actually bring family members closer".

The focus group attendees agreed that a child speaking to a mediator can help family dynamics. Reflecting the majority view, Aleah said that discussing child arrangements in CIM rather than directly between parents and children "keeps the family unit better". Grace felt that denying children the right to be heard in mediation "is just completely shutting down any voice that they have", which would stifle a child's willingness to express their views on other matters to their parents in the future. Joseph thought shutting down their voices might make children mistrustful or angry with their parents as they age.

Filtering and reframing

As discussed in Chapter Four, young people who had experienced CIM (but not the relationship professionals) raised filtering and reframing as allied benefits of hearing from children. That is the ability to filter, via a third party, messages that the young people realized might be hurtful for their parents to hear, coupled with the mediator's skills in reframing those messages more palatably to the parents. The relationship professionals described higher-level psychological benefits to young people of speaking to a neutral third party, whereas the young people were recounting their own experiences. Consequently, these benefits may not have come readily to the relationship professionals' minds.

The focus group participants also thought filtering messages through the mediator reduced the risk of parents distorting the child's words. Aleah thought filtering via a mediator is preferable because hearing an unpalatable message from the child directly "doesn't come across in the nicest way". The mediator's skill at reframing the message in a less hurtful way could, it was felt, help to calm the situation.

Whole family support on separation

Several relationship professionals emphasized that support for the parents was crucial for helping the child. Fran Clarkson said that supporting parents therapeutically to take a share of responsibility for and mourn the relationship breakdown "frees up the child" and could "take the weight off" their children's shoulders. Without this support, parents often become locked in high-conflict court cases. She favoured an early assessment of the parents' and child's needs and a referral to CIM, therapy or additional support for the parents and child.

Rosemary Allen strongly supported education for parents to understand their children's feelings. She felt this is the primary way children could be supported when parents separate. Similarly, Clara Farley thought it was futile to give counselling to children unless the parental environment was improved, including how the parents spoke about one another. She too, therefore, favoured a 'whole family' approach in which parents gained an understanding of how their actions affected their children. Margot Hendon supported this view. She felt that counselling for children alone, in the absence of parents taking responsibility for their actions, "could let some parents off the hook". She thought that there is an argument for compulsory parenting courses for separating parents to understand the child's perspective and improve their ability to listen to their children. The young people's comments were restricted to support for their peers rather than parents.

Conclusion

The relationship professionals and young people (in interviews and focus groups) were unanimous. Providing young people with an outlet to process their emotions when parents separate has benefits for their mental health and wellbeing. Most professionals and all young people agreed that CIM had a vital, although not exclusive, role to play in helping young people understand the legal processes, gain reassurance, and have their voices heard within the decision-making process.

A minority of relationship professionals felt that adults are the "judges" and that young people's involvement should be restricted to explaining the decisions made. Critics of such a position have argued that vesting decision-making power in the hands of the adults risks silencing children's voices and perpetuates an understanding of children as 'dependent and passive recipients of adults' actions' (Lee, 2001: 8).

Arguably, some of the benefits of hearing from young people – informing and reassuring, for example – could be provided within a therapeutic setting, and indeed some relationship professionals contended that a therapeutic intervention would be more effective. However, it is difficult to see how a traditional therapeutic intervention, although needed for some, could facilitate active and meaningful participation in the decision-making process central to upholding children's right to decisional privacy (Dimopoulos, 2021; 2022). A therapeutic intervention alone cannot guarantee that children's article 12 rights are realized. As Tobin (2013) rightly notes, article 12 radically reconceptualizes the adult–child decision-making relationship, requiring adults to work with children to create inclusive communication systems and processes that allow for children's views to be heard when parents separate; for children's views to be considered and treated seriously in decision-making processes; and requiring decision-makers to explain to children why certain decisions have been made. Only a mechanism that allows young people to participate at the heart of the decision-making process could come close to fulfilling our international obligations under article 12. In an era where parents are increasingly expected to settle matters in mediation, children's right to participate in the process must be respected consistently. For reasons that will unfold in the proceeding chapters, as currently conceptualized and practised, CIM falls short of the radical reconceptualization of children's rights that Tobin (2013) outlines. However, as an established practice, CIM has the potential to be a trailblazer for how an article 12 compliant system of support with respect for children's decisional privacy might be conceptualized and realized.

The staunch support for respecting the child's decisional privacy (Dimopoulos, 2021; 2022) expressed by the young people accords with Tobin's interpretation of article 12, that the measure does not simply give young people the right to an opportunity to influence the person who will make the decision. Instead, it requires that due weight be placed upon the child's views, anticipating that the views of a child of sufficient maturity and understanding will be determinative of his or her best interests (Tobin, 2015). Many young people believed they deserved a voice *and* a choice, although there was a recognition that the child's age and maturity must be weighed. The relationship professionals stopped short of this position. While recognizing the child's right to a voice in decision-making, most were careful to distinguish this from enabling young people to choose – voice, not choice. This position reflects the position taken by the English courts[2] – while the child has a right to have the opportunity to express their views and to be heard, this falls short of a right to self-determination (Gilmore, 2017: 230).

Establishing a framework of article 12 compliant direct support services of information, consultation, support and (where needed) representation for children and young people whose parents separate, accessible at the time of separation, and later as needed, as envisaged by the Family Solutions Group Report (2020) would go some way to meeting the information and support needs of young people whose parents separate as identified by the relationship professionals and young people. As noted in Chapter One, having first reconceptualized the approach to family separation so that its relational dimension is acknowledged and the autonomy of parents and their children in decision-making is rebalanced, we are analysing and reflecting on our data exploring CIM experiences through a UNCRC lens generally and article 12, in particular. In so doing, we are using Lundy's notion that article 12 rights involve space, voice, audience and influence for young people. Appendix II sets out Lundy's visualization of how a UNCRC article 12 model would work and the virtuous circle it would create. Appendix III provides a helpful checklist to ensure the model has been

---

[2]   *Re T (Abduction: Child's Objections to Return)* [2000] 2 FLR 192, at 203.

effectively operationalized. Acknowledging a young person's right to the space to express their views and operationalizing processes that facilitate their voices being heard are critical first steps to realizing an article 12 compliant model of child participation. Listening to and systematically according weight to those views in line with their evolving capacities is, as one relationship professional put it, "so powerful in so many ways" for young people. As others have emphasized, young people are involved in their parents' separation whether we involve them in the decision-making or not (Butler et al, 2002). Reframing our approach to and understanding of 'relational' autonomy as we propose places children at the heart of the decision-making per their article 12 rights. Systematically involving young people in *practice*, as the young people (and most relationship professionals) advocate, will require the mediation community (and parents) to embrace young people's right to be involved in *principle*. Reconceptualizing the process from one in which parental autonomy predominates to one in which the relational aspect is foregrounded may help the search for child-centred common ground. In Chapters Three, Four and Five, we draw on the Lundy model in our analysis of how well CIM fulfils article 12 as we examine our study's findings on the barriers to, experiences of and outcomes of CIM.

THREE

Entering Child-Inclusive Mediation: Barriers to Uptake

Introduction

Chapter One outlines the strong policy steer encouraging parents to resolve family law disputes out of court, ideally by mediation. Despite the UK's international obligations to afford young people mechanisms through which to express their views when parents separate, the lack of automatic rights for young people to be heard in mediation curtails their ability to exercise their article 12 rights and agency, creating an effective barrier to greater child–inclusive mediation (CIM) uptake. In addition to a general unawareness that children have such rights, we found four further critical impediments to greater uptake: a lack of consensus within the mediation profession and between the professionals and the public on the purpose(s) of CIM; systemic barriers such as costs and lack of awareness of accessible information about the CIM process for parents and children; practitioner confidence, in both the process and ability to deliver it well, and the critical gatekeeping roles of first the mediator and then the parents, which could prove impenetrable. This chapter will consider each of these impediments in turn.

The purpose of child-inclusive mediation

As outlined in Chapter Two, young people staunchly supported upholding children's right to be heard. We were therefore interested in the perspectives of the 20 mediators and 12 parents on the purpose of CIM in this regard, and whether these align with the views of the 39 young people whom we interviewed (N=20) or who were focus group participants (N=19).

Mediators

It is reasonable to expect that a process's purpose should be conceptualized, articulated and understood clearly by those trained and practising it. All the mediators interviewed had undertaken mandatory training to practise CIM. Three-quarters (15) had attended the compulsory update day. A further three were booked to attend, and two were undecided, acknowledging that non-attendance would cause their accreditation to lapse. However, our findings point to a lack of consensus between mediators on the purpose of CIM.

In 2012, when interviewed for the *Mapping* project, mediators unanimously agreed that the process should be child-focused (Barlow et al, 2017b: 181). However, not everyone thought it needed to be child-inclusive. Peter Young was not CIM trained but would bring a child consultant into the mediation process where needed. In 2012, he stated that young people's views are best incorporated through the parents: "The parents know their children best. They may have different views, but I think that parents are the best people to know their children." This 'parents know best' attitude had all but disappeared in the present sample. Only Norma Jones believed that consulting children indirectly via their parents was still "probably the best" way of eliciting children's views. She believed it is of "primary importance for the parents themselves to create a sort of atmosphere or environment for themselves to be consulting their children". In those circumstances, if parents were "working well together and collaborating", she thought it was usually unnecessary to involve the children directly. However, this was the minority view.

Save for Melanie Illingworth, who expressed unease at CIM "becoming the default position", the mediators we spoke to had made what Henry Sanderson described as the "intellectual shift" to "an understanding that the child's right to be heard needs to be at the centre of this process". There was less consensus, however, on why this should be so.

Progress

For some, progress towards a workable agreement was the primary purpose. For example, Jemma Green thought the child's involvement helps the mediator to pursue their own aims with the parents, enabling parents to agree to more workable child arrangements. Ann Potts, who had conducted two CIM processes, echoed this sentiment. She said we should not "drag children into grown-up conversations", but it was needed, "especially if the parents get stuck". Melanie Illingworth had strong reservations about involving children in mediation routinely because it may place pressure on the child. Nevertheless, she agreed that when a teenager has expressed a view to one parent, if repeating it to a neutral third party would solve the matter, "then fine".

Welfare

Some mediators detected a shift in emphasis regarding the perceived purpose of CIM in the mediation community over time. Marjorie Jenkins indicated that the "old" direct consultation model primarily assisted parents in deciding. In contrast, CIM was chiefly aimed at allowing young people to speak to somebody independently, whether they wanted their views to be fed back to their parents or not.

Reflecting findings from other research (Brown and Campbell, 2013: 195), for most mediators, progress was secondary to giving young people a voice and focusing on their welfare. Yvonne Newbury epitomized the majority view when she indicated that "the principal objective" of CIM is to give "children a chance to talk to somebody about how they are doing".

Dual purpose?

For many mediators, engaging in CIM has a 'dual purpose'. Reflecting similar comments from others, David Leighton thought its purpose lay in "upgrading the quality of decisions and parents' capacity to reach a conclusion" while giving young people a safe forum to offload. Henry Sanderson thought that eliciting children's views can help to "inform the parental decision-making", particularly when parents had become "stuck". However, he felt its broader purpose had "more to do with the child having been listened to properly". Acknowledging the centrality of the child's wellbeing, many mediators recognized that there were often ancillary benefits such as greater cooperation or reduced conflict, which, as Laura Gurney put it, is "a secondary extremely useful thing". Indeed, the two often worked in tandem. Sam Burns concluded that though he is working for the child's welfare, this is "hugely dependent on parents finding a way to get on board with a more collaborative, cooperative approach rather than a sort of competitive one that the court tends to encourage".

Children's rights

Only two of 20 mediators linked hearing from children explicitly to children's article 12 rights. One, Briony Simpson, had a background in advocacy for young people. She saw upholding young people's article 12 rights as "pivotal" and said this ran through the very core of all that she did in her practice. Unsurprisingly, she saw significantly more children in her practice than the other mediators interviewed. Conceptualizing children's participation through a rights lens in this way is likely to result in greater uptake of the process.

Parents

One of the most common challenges to children's meaningful participation in decision-making when parents separate is the tension between protection and participation rights. Parents who decline to involve their children in decision-making do so often because of a misguided perception that they are protecting their children (Barlow et al, 2017b; Barlow and Ewing, 2020: 38). However, far from protecting them, failure to hear from children may be disempowering or even harmful (Bell, 2016: 242). This may be particularly so in high-conflict cases since hearing from the children here can provide reassurance and support (Voice of the Child Advisory Group, 2015). Children tend to know more about the difficulties in their parents' relationship than parents give them credit for, and exclusion from involvement in decision-making causes them distress (Lansdown, 2011: 84; see also Kay-Flowers, 2019). While shielding young people from knowledge of the separation until the eleventh hour may spring from an understandable desire to protect children, it leads to poorer adjustment to the separation. However, this can be ameliorated when parents consider their child's views in decision-making (Kay-Flowers, 2019: 150). For parents who engaged in CIM, we were interested in what they perceived to be its purpose. Insights into why they chose to engage might inform attempts to address reticence in other parents, where appropriate. As with the mediators, there was a lack of consensus among the parents on CIM's purpose. Many thought it served several purposes simultaneously. In Australian research (Bell et al, 2012), parents disclosed multiple reasons for choosing CIM. Some were child-focused (the therapeutic benefit for the children in talking to someone, understanding their feelings, and giving them a voice in resolving the dispute). Others were primarily parent-focused (to gain assurance that what the child said to them reflected what they would say to an independent person and to help the other parent hear what the child wanted). There were overlaps with these child-focused and parent-focused reasons in the parents' responses in the present study.

Progress

Like the mediators, a minority of parents viewed CIM's primary purpose as making progress. Parents often reported involving the children when the parents had reached an impasse. Mary Dobson, for example, disclosed being "very against" seeking her children's opinions in the adult dispute initially but conceded the need to do so because she and the father were "going around in circles". Some parents were pragmatic. They knew that court proceedings were a real prospect if a decision was not reached, which they were keen to avoid.

Principle

None of the parents raised children's United Nations Convention of the Rights of the Child (UNCRC) rights, but for more than half, involving the children was a matter of principle, "the right thing to do" (Mark Bell), "morally the right thing to do" (Doug Henderson). Coming from this perspective, CIM was not a hard sell. Framing the offer to all parents of children of suitable age in terms of children's UNCRC rights, so that the decision becomes about why it would not be appropriate to allow *this* child to exercise their rights, may lead to greater uptake by parents who take a less principled stand on the matter than these parents.

Therapeutic benefits

Some parents sought CIM because its child-centred approach chimed with their own beliefs. Tanya Adams typified this view. CIM "ticked all of her boxes" because she wanted someone to deal with her children's emotions and for her children to feel empowered and that their opinions mattered. Half of the parents fell into this category, two-thirds of whom were mothers. If engaging mothers who value CIM's child-centred approach proves easier than engaging fathers, careful work may be needed to understand and address fathers' reticence, as outlined in the section on 'The imperative'.

Verification

Lastly, two-thirds of parents hoped the mediator would be an independent voice to confirm the veracity of the child's views. Many parents wanted the assurance that what their child said to them mirrored what they would say to an independent person. Alternatively, they hoped the process would help the other parent hear, assimilate and act upon the child's preferences. Much like parents who choose court because they think the judge will endorse their stance, these parents saw the mediator as an independent person in whom the child could confide to confirm to Parent A that what Parent B had been saying were the child's honest and independently reached views.

Ellen Foxton, for example, said that her ex-partner "would never have listened" to her, so "pretty much the only reason" for going to mediation was to allow the children to "put their point across ... so the mediator could hear it from the children and pass it on to [ex-partner]". The mediator, Sam Burns, recognized this tendency in parents. He cautioned that, in such instances, the way that the offer of mediation is framed and explained to the parents is critical because many parents seek CIM "because they anticipate that the children are going to confirm to you, this independent person, that they are right".

Many parents hoped involving the children would help the other parent agree to the interviewee's preferred contact regime. Several mediators confirmed that parents often sought CIM for this end, and expectations must be managed accordingly. This thinking by parents underscores the need for meticulous screening for suitability for CIM. There should be time with each parent individually to explore their motivation, particularly how they might respond if their child's views on contact do not align with their own.

Young people

As the mediators and parents hoped, the child's involvement had helped many families progress matters to agreement. However, the benefits to young people's wellbeing went far beyond this (as discussed in Chapters Four and Five). Regarding CIM's purpose, reflecting consistent messages from research in this jurisdiction (Neale, 2002; Walker and Lake-Carroll, 2014; Symonds et al, 2022) and abroad (Lansdown, 2001; Carson et al, 2018), young people viewed giving them a voice in the decision-making and respecting their views as imperative. Save for two focus group participants, none of the young people spoke of UNCRC rights or displayed an awareness of those rights. However, as discussed in Chapter Two, on principle and without exception, they felt that children should have the right to be involved, and that providing a mechanism by which children could exercise this right is CIM's foundational purpose.

The young people highlighted secondary purposes, including providing an outlet to help them understand the process better and adjust to the separation, a mechanism for getting painful messages across to their parents and assisting the mediator in grasping the child's true feelings.

Barriers to access to information and support

Before discussing the barriers to greater uptake of CIM, it is worth noting that, consistent with the findings of other research (Barlow et al, 2017a; Symonds et al, 2022; Family Solutions Children's Group, 2023), our young people participants had encountered significant barriers to accessing the information and support they needed more generally when parents separated. A minority disclosed poor experiences when trying to elicit support from professionals to whom they ought to have been able to turn at crisis points, such as teachers, GPs and the police, indicating a need for better training for professionals on the impact of parental separation on children. Several focus group participants said that internet searches had been unhelpful. From Google searches, Louise discovered that as a child of divorced parents, she was more likely to get diabetes, drop out of education or go to prison, but nothing that had helped her. Others disclosed stumbling across the information and support they needed. As Aleah explained, "Because there is no set-up in place for young people, it's down to luck." Farah said that it was "pure luck" that she had found the National Youth Advocacy Service (NYAS) when she had been given access to a school computer. She reflected that, but for her work on the Family Justice Young People's Board, had she been going through it again, "I still wouldn't know where to start, I wouldn't know who I could talk to, can I talk to ChildLine? Do I qualify as such to talk to them? Is the situation severe enough, or [can I speak to] NYAS again?"

The focus group participants whose parents litigated bemoaned the lack of continuity of professionals in the case. In separate cases, two young women spoke of "cultural disadvantages" and unconscious biases and assumptions about the "family dynamics" of their Asian families. Each said the professionals involved failed to take their genuinely held preference to live with their respective fathers seriously. Craig disclosed challenges associated with accessing appropriate information and support in rural areas.

The focus group participants had two primary solutions to the lack of accessible information and support. The first was access to a universal, well-publicized website that would become the 'go-to' source of information and support for young people on parental separation. As Aleah said, "there is no direction. I think that's the problem, and I think having one place where everyone can start is a really good idea".

The second was more information and support for young people in schools. This might be through improved school counselling, pastoral support or peer support for general reassurance. As Ruby put it, having someone who could say, "This happened to me too, that would help a lot ... just to make [you] feel like [you are] less alone and that [you are] not the only person that these sorts of things happen to." However, schools should only be informed of parental separation with the young person's authority as school may be the only place, as Farah said, where children "can still feel some sense of normality". They felt this was particularly important given the stigma that still attaches to divorce in some communities. Existing support provision in schools was felt to be "a lottery", and some, like Louise, felt badly let down by the lack of compassion and understanding they had experienced from most of their teachers. Louise felt that teachers needed better awareness of the mental health impact of parental separation on young people.

The focus group participants and young people we interviewed staunchly supported universal relationship education lessons on parental separation. Arming young people with information on processes and rights would make the process less intimidating for those whose parents subsequently separate. It would allow peers to support one another. Despite its prevalence, there was considerable frustration that parental separation is not covered adequately in schools. Ruby felt that schools have a valuable role in normalizing the prevalence of parental separation and young people's rights to be heard in decision-making. She saw the lack of teaching in this area as a "fundamental problem". Aleah was frustrated that personal, social, health and economic education (PSHE) lessons cover "uncommon" experiences such as teen pregnancy, which would affect only a few students, but not parental separation even though it is "so, so common". In a different focus group, Becky expressed a similar sentiment: "We study about not taking drugs, and healthy eating and relationships ... but even though divorce and separation is [sic] so common, we never learn about it at school ... so, it's seen as something different from the norm."

The Department for Education guidance requires teachers to be 'aware of common "adverse childhood experiences" (such as family breakdown …) and when and how these may be affecting any of their pupils' (DfE, 2019: para 102). In fulfilling this requirement, the message from the focus group participants was that schools should not shy away from teaching about parental separation since, as mentioned in Chapter Three, children are more resilient than adults think and may benefit from learning about it.

Barriers to greater uptake of child-inclusive mediation

Article 12 places a positive and unqualified duty upon State Parties to afford children an appropriate and safe space to express their views on matters concerning them. It is the weight placed upon those views that must be considered per a child's age and maturity. In upholding our international obligations towards children, there is a positive duty 'to invite and encourage their input rather than simply acting as a recipient of views if children happen to provide them' (Lundy, 2007: 934). However, our research revealed significant barriers to ensuring that children are invited and encouraged to participate in CIM systematically, in line with our international obligations.

In the following sections, we outline some barriers to greater uptake of CIM and suggest how those might be overcome. The young people we spoke to were capable, resilient 'beings' (not simply 'becomings') (Diduck and Kaganas, 2012: 504). Nevertheless, mediators felt that in addition to a general lack of awareness of CIM and systemic barriers such as costs, parental reluctance to involve children in what they viewed as adult decision-making went to the heart of parental concerns about facilitating young people's meaningful participation. However, our evidence indicates that practitioners are the first gatekeepers to children engaging in CIM, with practitioners' lack of confidence, either in the process or in their ability as child-inclusive mediators, a significant hurdle. Having interviewed some of the mediators previously (Barlow et al, 2017b), the confidence of many had increased over time, leading to changes in how mediators framed the offer. Those who consciously framed the offer as a right for children found that parents were more likely to accept.

Awareness

Lack of awareness of CIM is a significant obstacle to greater uptake. Among adults, this lack of awareness starts even with the professionals working with separating families. The mediator, Melanie Illingworth, noted that many lawyers are unaware that CIM is available to clients and their children.

Awareness of CIM was low among the parents and young people interviewed. Only four of the 12 parents and one of the 20 children had heard of it before the parents engaged in mediation, the child through school. Two further children had heard of mediation and assumed that children would be involved. In 2018, the Family Mediation Council (FMC) amended its national 'Standards Framework' to require mediators to explain CIM to prospective clients. This should ensure that parents are routinely informed once they have approached a mediator. However, work is needed to enhance CIM awareness in the general population, including non-legal professionals (for example, teachers and GPs) who are on the front line with separating families. Training to professionals such as teachers on the availability of mediation, including CIM, is much needed and appreciated. As a teacher who had received training said, "Very often [when parents separate], it's just been, 'Oh, I'm sorry to hear that' … We have never really been able to say, 'Have you considered mediation? … Here's a leaflet that might be of some use to you.' We have not had that tool in our toolkit" (Barlow and Ewing, 2020: 15). Gatekeepers within the wider community, as well as parents and children, need greater awareness of CIM. Dedicated PSHE lessons on children's rights when parents separate, as strongly advocated for by the young people we spoke to, would help to address the lack of awareness of CIM among young people.[1] The dedicated 'go to' website for which the focus group participants called could also help raise awareness. The website should include a space for parents, children and professionals who work on the frontline of parental separation, such as teachers or GPs (Family Solutions Group, 2020: 49).

Costs

We spoke to parents who had engaged in the process and had overcome any reservations about costs, but several saw costs as a disincentive, as discussed further in Chapter Four. Even some young people were concerned that the ability to speak to the mediator they had enjoyed might be unavailable to children of less affluent parents.

Despite Henry Sanderson noting that most mediators have made the "intellectual shift" needed to embrace hearing from children, he concluded that "the impediments in terms of funding are so great that it is difficult to see how they can actually then put that into practice". This echoed Marjorie Jenkins' concerns. She felt that the CIM update day had enthused (or re-enthused) mediators to undertake CIM. However, mediators received a "double message" on the update day that they should be seeing children, while acknowledging that no (public) money is available to pay for this. This, she recognized, was a significant obstacle to greater uptake. Some mediators committed to CIM had begun offering it free of

---

[1]　In response to this, in a recent collaboration between the authors and colleagues at NYAS and National Association of Child Contact Centres, PSHE Association quality mark assured teaching resources on children's rights when parents separate for secondary schools (*The Rights Idea?*) and primary schools (*Rosie's Story*) have been developed. Both have been adapted for use in the Curriculum for Wales, with the support of the Welsh Government.

charge. Others had done so, mindful of needing at least three CIM cases over three years to keep their accreditation (FMC, 2014: 6.3(b)). This would not be sustainable long term. Removing the 'stumbling block' of funding will be key to achieving greater uptake, and we make recommendations to this end in Chapter Six.

Lawyers and mediators as gatekeepers

The traditional route into mediation pre-Legal Aid, Sentencing and Punishment of Offenders Act 2012 (LASPO) was through solicitor referral and could still be a key route for privately funded cases. As outlined in Chapter One, the LASPO changes, which removed public funding from most family cases, caused a haemorrhaging of mediation starts in the immediate aftermath of LASPO, with starts never having fully recovered.

Several lawyer and non-lawyer mediators viewed lawyers' attitudes as an obstacle to greater uptake of mediation, including CIM. Jennifer Eccles felt that lawyers are "massively incentivized to litigate". Briony Simpson thought there was a cohort of lawyers who, for monetary reasons, believed that court or solicitor negotiations were always preferable to mediation. Melanie Illingworth noted that many lawyers are unaware of CIM as a process available to clients and their children.

Practitioner confidence

Practitioners' lack of confidence in the process or their ability to conduct CIM was a potent obstacle to greater uptake of CIM. As recognized elsewhere, professional anxiety about burdening young people with the adult conflict from which the system should shield them, when coupled with cost restraints, can result in failure to uphold children's right to participate (JUSTICE, 2022: para 3.58).

The FMC introduced compulsory update training for all CIM-trained mediators in 2018. Several mediators reported that this had boosted mediators' confidence and, as a result, uptake. When interviewed for the *Mapping* project in 2012, Maria Ingram indicated that CIM was "something we often flag up" in the first meeting with the client, yet it was rarely pursued. In Maria's case, lack of practice led to a lack of confidence in her ability and the process. She said that because of legal aid cost restraints, she did little CIM work for years, "and I guess as the years went by ... I [lacked] confidence, and it didn't really feel like the thing that you really had to do". While some experienced CIM mediators felt they had not learned much during the update day, less experienced CIM mediators, like Maria, reported that it had had a "significant impact" on their confidence in the process and ability to conduct it well. Maria became aware of the pressing need to involve children and the willingness of parents to accept an offer when framed positively. By 2020, she saw children monthly. She attributed the increase to a conscious change in how she presented CIM to the parent. She told us, "I thought people didn't want to do it, but ... if you present it in a certain way, and you present it as the thing that you do as part of the mediation process, if you normalize it, then actually clients do want to do it." Maria's experience resonated with the views of more experienced child-inclusive mediators. Marjorie Jenkins pointed to anecdotal evidence that some mediators had found the initial training for CIM insufficient and consequently conducted few mediations, which meant what little confidence they had, ebbed. Marjorie felt that attendance at the update day had "re-energized" many mediators and, while some are sceptical, "others are more prepared to go out and just make it part of their conversation about what they do".

Jemma Green saw mediators' lack of familiarity with the process as a significant barrier. Reflecting this observation, Audrey Rogerson attributed the substantial increase in the proportion of cases in which she met the child since 2012 to "familiarity with the idea ... I think it does really help to be able to say that it is an expectation ... as something that we would routinely offer unless there's a reason not to". Audrey explained that, following some additional intensive training, she and her colleagues decided to reframe the offer of CIM to clients, leading to a substantial increase in uptake. Rather than asking, "Would you be willing for us to talk to your child?" they chose to "turn it around and say, 'We see children as a matter of course, are you happy for us to offer this opportunity to your child?'" When parents are reluctant, they follow this up with, "That's absolutely fine, but would you be willing to check?" While an invitation direct to the child would be better still, this reframing of the offer was critical to greater uptake. Normalizing the offer like this respects the child's right to 'space' and 'voice'.

Confident mediators are likely to frame the offer of CIM so that it is more likely to be accepted. How the offer of mediation is framed to a prospective client in the initial telephone call to a mediation service can dictate how likely the client is to accept the offer (Sikveland and Stokoe, 2016). Similarly, how the offer of CIM is explained to a parent and how the mediator "frames the task of meeting the children" (Sam Burns) is critical. Patricia Todd, who estimated that she had seen more than 75 young people in CIM, tells parents, "One of the benefits of mediation, as opposed to the court, is that your child can have a voice, you know, they can come to talk to the mediator, and that's a really good opportunity." Framing it as a positive opportunity for young people increased parents' willingness to try the process in Patricia's view. Practitioners confident in the process and their ability reported a shift in parents' attitudes and willingness to undertake the process. Sam Burns, who tells clients that it is "normative for me to meet ... children aged ten and over", said that the increase in uptake of CIM in his practice "could be [because of] the way I put it across, that I own it more". His practice had shifted in recent years. Rather than viewing CIM as a "possible add-on" to the process, his mindset is now, "Well, why wouldn't you want me to see your children? ... It's more of a sort of an opt-out [option]. ... That's the change in my approach, and that's how I sell it if you like." Since parents may see the benefits of involving children generally but be reluctant concerning their children, normalizing the offer of CIM so that it is explained as a routine part of the process may address parents' hesitancy (Brown and Campbell, 2013: 195).

Audrey Rogerson explained that confidence builds as mediators experience the process and witness the positive outcomes for children, including that children welcome it and do not find it a burden. She said, "It's the belief of the mediator, because it doesn't matter how good the 'script' is, you have got to believe [in] it ... to be authentic with the parents ... and that comes [with] experience."

What then of the mediators who conducted few mediations? Why was this the case? Six of the 20 mediators interviewed had consulted with a child in five or fewer cases since training.[2] All six had been interviewed as part of the *Mapping* project.

For the six mediators who had conducted few child-inclusive cases, reasons for not engaging in CIM more regularly were evenly split between lack of confidence in their ability to conduct the process and in the process itself; the latter either because of concerns about the possible risks to the child or ambivalence about the process.

Experienced CIM mediators who are Professional Practice Consultants noted a reticence among their less experienced consultees to see children. Yvonne Newbury attributed this to consultees' lack of confidence and fear that they might make things worse. We found evidence to support this among those

---

[2] A survey conducted for the Voice of the Child Report indicated that approximately one-third of mediators registered with the FMC had trained in CIM, but of those who responded to the survey, most (70 per cent) conducted less than 10 CIMs per year (Voice of the Child Advisory Group, 2015).

who had conducted few child consultations. David Leighton, for example, had trained in CIM but had not seen any children directly, preferring to refer children-only cases to a more experienced (male) colleague who was "better at it" than he felt he was. He thought it was one thing to "have a go" at mediating financial cases if that was "within your skillset", but to "have a go" at speaking to children was not appropriate, for him at least.

Maria Ingram felt that practitioner confidence is a particular issue for male mediators as this can be "outside their comfort zone". She was sympathetic to what her male colleagues said about "the additional complexities because of their gender". David Leighton acknowledged the difficulty of, in his view, a "crusty old git" like him doing this work. However, he referred cases to his male colleague who regularly saw children, recognizing aptitude and experience, rather than gender, should be the deciding criteria.

While the FMC Code of Practice mandates that '[a]ll children and young people aged 10 and above should be offered the opportunity to have their voices heard directly during the Mediation, if they wish' (FMC, 2018: 6.6.1),[3] the practitioners proved effective gatekeepers. Kirsty Oliver had conducted very few CIM cases. She said that she tended to tell parents about CIM where appropriate, and it was on these occasions parents had accepted the offer, yet she had seen very few children. Similarly, Melanie Illingworth had seen very few children since qualifying five years before the interview. She saw no need for greater uptake of CIM, viewing it as "an optional bolt-on". Briony Simpson was frustrated at the update day with the number of CIM-trained mediators whose view was still, "I just don't know when you do it". She felt there was a strong need for Professional Practice Consultants to challenge this thinking

---

[3]   Identical wording appeared in the previous draft of the Code of Practice (FMC, 2016: 5.7.2).

among their consultees. She argued that a lack of confidence among CIM-trained mediators made them reluctant to offer it to parents, and the consequent lack of experience meant they had not had the opportunity to witness the positive impact it can have on children.

Sam Burns felt that while historically it had been normative for experienced mediators to qualify to consult children, the enhanced CIM training may function as a disincentive for ambivalent mediators because of the cost, effort and expectation of professional competence. Briony Simpson welcomed that reaccreditation requirements would "weed out" mediators who had trained to conduct the process but whose mindsets had remained litigious rather than child-focused and inclusive. The reaccreditation requirements may lead some mediators to let their accreditation lapse. Both Caroline Underwood and David Leighton indicated that since their practice was primarily financial cases, consulting with children would take them out of their "comfort zone". Caroline reflected that the interview had shown her that she was "not qualified to do" CIM. She said she probably would not attend the update day and would let her accreditation lapse. David's view was, "If I am trying to do the best by the client, why would I do it incompetently when there's someone who can do it with much more experience than me?" It seemed likely that, along with five other mediators interviewed, his accreditation would lapse by default given the lack of CIM work he undertook.

Parents as gatekeepers

Parental gatekeeping has been identified as a strong barrier to greater uptake of child-inclusive practice, with parents seeing the merits of the process for children generally but not for their children (Brown and Campbell, 2013: 195). While, as outlined earlier, the reticence of some mediators proved an initial hurdle, all but one practitioner cited the reluctance of at least one parent as a barrier to greater uptake. A desire to shield the children from what they viewed as an adult dispute drove parental reluctance to engage in CIM. Paternalistic mindsets; failure to see the need to consult children; fear of what the child might say; the need for both parents' consent; the emotional readiness of the parents to engage in the process; and (as mentioned earlier) costs were also effective barriers. One practitioner, Melanie Illingworth, said that as making progress was central to why many parents choose CIM, if this could not be assured, many chose not to authorize the mediator to invite the children.

Protection

Many mediators concurred with Bella Morris' view that "The biggest barrier is [that] the parents are the gatekeepers. ... There are a lot of parents who believe they are protecting their children by not involving them [or] giving them any information." As Kirsty Oliver put it, the desire to "protect their children from the kind of adult world" was the most frequently cited reason the practitioners gave for parental reticence to involve their children. She empathized with parents who viewed bringing their child to a lawyer's office as "scary". This underscores the careful thought that needs to go into both the offer to the parent and child, and the ambience of the setting for CIM, as discussed further in Chapter Four. Kirsty was the only mediator to highlight that the child, as well as the parents, might be reticent. Others stressed that once the parents saw the merit in involving the child, the child would usually accept the invitation.

Several mediators noted that while parents might couch their resistance in terms of a desire to protect the child from the adult dispute, often, these parents seemed to have quite paternalistic parenting approaches.

Many parents disclosed that they had indeed been reluctant to involve the child initially, as explained by Rose Enstone, who said that she had been "a bit nervous" and "slightly tentative" as she did not want to "drag [the children] into what was a painful family episode". Given what she perceived as their father's forceful character, Rose was concerned about whether the children would feel comfortable speaking up. She saw the gender of the mediator (a man) as a positive benefit in her circumstances. She overcame her reluctance to involve the children because she saw the mediator as "a kindred spirit" who had "couched it as a nice way; that the children could for once be allowed to actually express their emotions surrounding the ... breakdown and have a say". As discussed in the earlier section on 'Practitioner confidence', the mediator couching the offer positively assuaged the concerns of Rose and other parents.

Paternalism

Mediators highlighted parents' mindsets as a critical determinant of their suitability for CIM. If parents have rigid ideas about the arrangements and lack the "psychological capacity to be able to make the process a positive one for their children" (Jennifer Eccles), they may be unsuitable or at least children's expectations would need to be carefully managed. The mediators indicated that parents with inflexible mindsets often are not open to involving their children. As Kirsty Oliver said, "Some parents ... maybe don't want to think of giving their children any self-determination." Parental reluctance stemming from paternalistic attitudes proved some of the thorniest cases for mediators. Most felt that the case should be deemed unsuitable for CIM if the parents cannot prioritize their child's needs and are not "psychologically in a position to take heed of what a child is saying" (Norma Jones). Others felt that the children of such parents could benefit from having an outlet to express their feelings, even if the mediator needs to manage the child's expectations around outcomes.

Only two of the 20 children interviewed had been unhappy with the outcome of mediation because they felt that their father had ignored their views. It is impossible to predict accurately how a parent might respond to an unpalatable message from their child. However, for parents with very fixed ideas, who seem incapable of moderating their stance, whatever the child may say, CIM may not be appropriate unless there are other likely benefits for the child. As outlined in Chapter Four, there may be benefits from the child's perspective that would make it worthwhile proceeding, so we would not endorse a blanket ban on CIM, even in these circumstances.

The imperative

Yvonne Newbury felt that many parents underestimated the effect of the separation on their children, so they failed to see the value of including them. She saw a need to change parents' perception of CIM's purpose, so they would begin to value their children having an independent voice in the process, regardless of whether this affects the outcome. She felt the parental reluctance could be overcome by a gentle general introduction to the concept individually in the Mediation and Information Assessment Meeting so that the parent "can start to think about it", with the assurance that the matter would be revisited in the first joint meeting. It also required the mediator to frame the offer positively: "The more confident you are … about the benefits of … speaking to children … that does help to shift the parents' reluctance." Practitioners' confidence in the process builds parents' confidence in it.

Clear information and explanations of the process for parents, reinforced periodically, can also help to overcome parental reluctance. Jemma Green explained that parental reluctance "can be addressed by the way we speak about the process … if we are very clear at various points that it's not about the child making decisions".

In the earlier *Mapping* project, most parents were also extremely cautious about involving their children. Ernest, one of the two (of 56) parents who had experienced CIM, resolved the issue of which school his daughter should attend through

CIM. Nevertheless, he concluded that "there's better ways of focusing on the child than actually bringing them to mediation. I think it puts them in a very difficult position" (Barlow et al, 2017b: 135). A decade later, increased practitioner confidence in the process (and their ability to conduct it effectively) seemed to affect parents' willingness to engage positively. One parent, Trevor Cox, told us he was initially "dead against the idea" of CIM but had overcome his reluctance after several conversations with the mediator, who had framed the offer positively and outlined the benefits of the process, allaying his concerns. Having engaged in the process, Trevor concluded that "without a doubt ... you have to involve children".

Fear

As one of the relationship professionals, Jacob Beardsley, pointed out (see Chapter Two), mediators need to acknowledge how disconcerting it can be for a parent to give their child a voice in the process, thereby risking the child criticizing their parenting or choosing against them. Echoing this view, several mediators indicated that parental fear that the child might criticize or reject them is a formidable obstacle. As Angela Brown said, parental reluctance stems from "an unspoken fear that maybe a child would make a judgment or criticize or choose".

Jemma Green highlighted the meticulous preparatory work needed with fearful parents, noting that without this, some parents will be unable to "fully hear the feedback". Engaging with parents at their own pace to acknowledge and alleviate parents' understandable fears and gently explain the benefits to children of having their voices heard could, in the view of several mediators, help to alleviate parental concerns.

One parent's reluctance

Since it is a voluntary process, one parent's refusal to attend is an undoubted barrier to greater uptake of mediation (Barlow et al, 2017b: 90). This continues to be an obstacle, including to CIM. Echoing similar sentiments from other mediators, Yvonne Newbury concluded that "one parent's reluctance is the biggest obstacle to it".

The Voice of the Child Report recommended that Gillick competent children should be able to have their voice heard by a suitably qualified practitioner if they so wish, without the need for parental consent, and that the consent of one parent only should suffice where the child is deemed not to be Gillick competent (Voice of the Child Advisory Group, 2015: Recommendations 19 and 20). The JUSTICE Report calls for a 'system-wide presumption that all children should be offered the opportunity to participate in processes which concern them, both in and out of court, in an age-appropriate way' (JUSTICE, 2022: 4). However, it points to the difficulty of gaining access to a child in the absence of parental consent and, since mediation is a voluntary process, the likelihood that one parent will withdraw from the process if their consent is bypassed. The Report therefore calls for better education and information for parents rather than any form of mandation (JUSTICE, 2022: 3.75–3.77).

The FMC has resisted calls for reform to the process of engaging the child. Children participate voluntarily with the informed consent and support of both parents (or those holding parental responsibility) (FMC, 2014: 40; FMC, 2018: 6.62). As a result, one parent's reluctance will stymie the process. As Sam Burns said, "given that one is in a voluntary domain ... I don't think you can [impose CIM] ... the bottom line is you have got to have an agreement of both parties, don't you?"

Emotional readiness

Several mediators pointed to a lack of emotional readiness to engage in CIM as the root cause of many parents' reluctance. Just as parents need to be emotionally ready to mediate (Barlow et al, 2017a; 2017b), they must be emotionally ready to engage in CIM. As Kirsty Oliver told us, if parents come to mediation when "at the 'blame game' [stage]" when they are still "emotionally quite vulnerable", the thought of involving the children "is just ... a step too far".

As found elsewhere (Barlow et al, 2017b), Kirsty thought that parental anger abates with time, and they may then be more willing for their child's voice to be heard. Angela Brown said that parents' capacity can diminish immediately after separation. Preoccupied with their own needs, parents find it challenging to comprehend what their children might be experiencing at this crisis point. This temporary state must be distinguished from parents who lack capacity altogether. In the former instance, as Barlow et al (2017b) recommend, Angela thought putting temporary arrangements in place might be necessary. Marjorie Jenkins felt that parental capacity to hear and take on board the child's views may "evolve" as the parent begins to trust the process. Jemma Green underscored the importance of waiting until the parents are emotionally capable of taking on board the child's feedback before engaging in CIM. As Patricia Todd summed up, CIM is most likely to achieve positive outcomes where parents are egalitarian, the separation has not been too wounding, life has moved on, and the parents are focused on the child's happiness.

Kirsty Oliver suggested that making CIM an opt-out rather than an opt-in process might concentrate the minds of parents who would otherwise be reluctant to allow their children to have a voice, resulting in greater uptake.

Other reasons cited by practitioners for parental reluctance to involve their children included the perceived unsuitability of children on the autistic spectrum and, as previously discussed, cost.

Policy restraints

Lastly, many mediators recognized that embedding article 12 compliant processes requires wholesale support from the government and policy makers and appropriate funding. Henry Sanderson lamented the absence of children's voices generally within private family law processes. Others felt that progress was unlikely until a government minister grasped the imperative of upholding children's participation rights.

Echoing similar sentiments from many of the mediators, Audrey Rogerson made a plea to policy makers and those who hold the purse strings for better funding for CIM. Bella Morris doubted the political will to take responsibility towards these children seriously, as the government is preoccupied with other issues.

Henry Sanderson felt that there had been a failure on the part of the government to educate and (where appropriate) support parents in making decisions. He supported the rollout of a 'Mediation in Mind' model (Barlow and Ewing, 2020). He thought such a model, which had, embedded in a mediation process, "proper triage, proper information and guidance, proper counselling and proper education about the role of separating parents" was critical to "get to where we need to get to".

Conclusion

There was a lack of consensus among practitioners and parents on the purpose of CIM. Many practitioners and parents viewed it as primarily a vehicle for progressing matters, especially when negotiations had reached a stalemate. Consulting young people to break a deadlock risks putting a child under pressure to decide and disappoint one parent. Therefore, careful screening is needed to judge how a disappointed parent will respond. Only consulting the child if an impasse is reached is a derogation of our international obligations. It fails to value children's internationally recognized rights. It does not acknowledge the value of hearing from children and the myriad of benefits children derive from the process, which go far beyond resolving the presenting issue (as discussed in Chapter Four).

The children of parents who do not reach an impasse would be denied the opportunity to enjoy those benefits.

Most mediators spoke of the twin goals of progressing and improving child welfare and outcomes. This duality of purpose is not inherently amiss. Making progress is a desirable end, particularly if the agreement reached has incorporated the child's wishes and feelings and will further the child's welfare. However, inviting children to participate for this reason alone does not meet our international obligations. It fails to uphold a child's 'decisional privacy' rights (Dimopoulos, 2021). Only a rights-framed approach to hearing from children could hope to achieve this end. Progress must become an ancillary benefit, not the primary goal.

While practitioners cited parental reluctance as an effective barrier to greater uptake of CIM, the evidence pointed to the practitioners themselves as the first line of defence. A lack of confidence in their ability to conduct the process effectively and, to a lesser extent, the process itself stymies greater uptake. Attendance at the compulsory update day has gone some way to re-energizing practitioners and persuading them of the merits of the process. It is imperative that initial and ongoing training is framed around children's rights to be heard and the benefits of doing so. Just as the extent to which judges can engage with understandings of children as rights bearers depends on their convictions (Dimopoulos, 2022: 69), so too do mediators need to be convinced that children's participation is a rights issue. The 'relational family autonomy' approach that we advocate puts young people at the heart of decision-making, moving them from the side-lines to centre stage, as we have argued elsewhere (Ewing et al, 2015). Unless the mediation community coalesces around a common purpose for CIM, the increase in sorely needed uptake will be slow to materialize.

Parental reluctance to involve children appears to stem primarily from a misguided wish to protect children from what is viewed as an adult dispute. Presenting the offer to parents positively within a children's rights framework should ensure that some of this reluctance falls away. Underscoring the relational and familial aspects of decision-making may help parents come to mediation with a problem-solving, child-inclusive focus, making it more likely that sustainable agreements acceptable to parents and their children will be reached. Since the evidence showed that parents who accepted the *principle* of child involvement readily were more likely to take it up, placing respect for children's autonomous decision-making (in line with their emerging capacities) at the heart of the mediation process, as we propose, should increase uptake. Furthermore, it should ensure that the parents consider the child's views meaningfully. Acknowledging children as rights-bearing subjects with interests distinct from those of their parents (Dimopoulos, 2021) would also help address some of these systemic barriers to greater inclusion of children within mediation and other forms of non-court processes. From this perspective, the question becomes *how* not *whether* children participate in the process and state funding should flow accordingly. In Chapter Six, we revisit the findings to explore how reconceptualizing the purpose of CIM through a children's rights framework might address some of the identified barriers to greater uptake.

FOUR

Experiences of
Child-Inclusive Mediation

Introduction

In the earlier *Mapping* study, we found mediation processes to be child-focused but rarely child-inclusive, with children's interests and views represented indirectly only via their parents (Ewing et al, 2015; Barlow et al, 2017b). Just as children's wishes and feelings tend 'to be represented by proxy, adult-filtered accounts' (Stalford and Hollingsworth, 2020: 1055) in court proceedings, our earlier study found that in the main, children's wishes and feelings were brought into mediation via the parents. Since the young people we interviewed for the *Healthy Relationship Transitions* (*HeaRT*) project had expressed their views directly to the mediator, we were interested in how they had experienced the process. Did their active participation in decision-making have the mental health and wellbeing benefits the relationship professionals identified? Could child-inclusive mediation (CIM) be a 'powerful tool' in enabling young people's right to be heard as 'equal partner[s] in a family', as mediation practitioners such as Henry Sanderson argued? Was hearing from young people in the decision-making process associated with a high level of accommodation of parental separation, as others have found (Kay-Flowers, 2019: 147)? Murch (2018: 110) suggests that young people at a time of crisis such as parental separation need a 'passage agent' who acts as a supportive guide to children when families break down to help them traverse the strange and unfamiliar territory of family life post-parental separation. Could mediators be a source of support to young people, a valuable 'passage agent' to help them navigate the changes in their family lives?

This chapter sets out our findings, first concerning differences between mediators in how the CIM is conducted. It outlines the views of the young people in the focus groups and interviews on age restrictions on CIM. It then explores how satisfied young people (and parents) were with the process of CIM before considering satisfaction with outcomes in Chapter Five. We consider the practical arrangements for hearing from young people against the first two of Lundy's (2007: 933) four-stage model of an article 12 compliant approach: 'space' (children must have the opportunity to express a view) and 'voice' (children must be facilitated to express their views) which taken together make up the first limb of article 12, the child's right to express an opinion. In considering young people's experiences and satisfaction with the process of CIM, we will discuss whether children felt listened to (the third limb, 'audience') and, if so, how this helped them. We discuss the fourth requirement, 'influence' (acting upon the child's views, as appropriate), in Chapter Five. The third and fourth limbs deal with Part 2 of article 12, giving the child's views due weight. In Chapter Two, we discussed relationship professionals and young people's views on the principle of giving young people a voice in decision-making when parents separate. In this chapter, we discuss the feedback from young people who were given a voice.

The process of child-inclusive mediation

We first explore the differences in the process experienced by young people, including how the process was explained to them; whether they met the mediator online or offline; whether they met the same mediator as their parents; how what was to be fed back to the parents was agreed and how feedback was given (to the parents separately or jointly and in the presence of the children or not). Mediators often had strong views on the merits of the process they adopted, with most preferring a model in which they met with both the parents and the child. However, there were few differences in reported satisfaction rates of parents or children between processes in which the children met with the same mediator as their parents compared to when children saw a different mediator or child consultant.

The offer: 'space'

Research shows that most of all, young people with experience of the family law system following parental separation want 'space to speak and more effective listening to their views and experiences' (Carson et al, 2018: ix). Arguably, to be fully article 12 compliant, the child should be involved from the outset in deciding whether CIM is appropriate (Dennison, 2010: 176). Lundy (2007: 933) argues that while elsewhere in the United Nations Convention of the Rights of the Child (UNCRC), State Parties are required to 'take appropriate measures to ensure' or 'use their best efforts to ensure', article 12 requires them to 'assure' to the child a means of having their voice heard. This indicates a duty to take proactive steps to encourage children to express their views (should they wish to do so). As General Comment No. 12 clarifies, 'shall assure' is a 'legal term of special strength, which leaves no leeway for State parties' discretion' (UNCRC General Comment No. 12, 2009: para 19). Article 12 requires mediators to provide mechanisms by which young people's voices can be heard and taken seriously within mediation. Therefore, article 12 compliant services must first ensure children can express a view ('space') (Lundy, 2007: 933). However, in addition to systemic barriers, practitioners and parents proved formidable gatekeepers to children exercising their article 12 rights, as outlined in Chapter Three. There was no sense that mediators ensured that *all* children capable of forming a view were allowed to express their views as required by article 12 or even that *all* children over the age of ten were given this opportunity (FMC, 2018: 6.6.1). Indeed, even for those children that had taken part in CIM, there was no consistent system for inviting them.

The Family Mediation Council (FMC)'s Standards Framework (2014), which includes updates concerning CIM made in 2018, sets out what must take place before the child is invited to attend (FMC, 2014: 6.4e) and states that young people may respond to an invitation directly or via a parent or carer (FMC, 2014: 6.4h). However, it is silent on who should invite the child – the mediator or the parent? Data is available concerning the invitation mode on 17 of the 20 mediators. All confirmed that they contacted the child by letter, e-mail or telephone to invite them to mediation. A further two mentioned that they wrote to the children following the child's meeting with the mediator. While memories were sometimes sketchy, the 20 young people we interviewed said that the initial invitation to CIM had come from someone other than the mediator. One was asked whether they wished to attend by the Family Court Adviser (as the parents were already within proceedings), one by their resident grandparent and the rest by one or both parents (11 by their mother, three by their father and four by both parents). Two young people recalled receiving an e-mail or letter from the mediator (both following an explanation from their respective mothers). Only one child recalled receiving a leaflet explaining the process, with another indicating that they were given written information at the meeting. In the parent sample, we interviewed the parent(s) of the child(ren) interviewed in all but one case. The parents confirmed the child's account of events, with all but one parent indicating that they (rather than the mediator) had told the child about CIM, three indicating that the mediator followed this up with a letter. In *Mapping*, there was evidence that one partner would be more likely to reject or be suspicious of mediation when the invitation came from the ex-partner rather than the mediator directly (Barlow et al, 2017b: 91). A mediator in the present study, Kirsty Oliver, felt that "a letter dropping on your mat" from a mediator unannounced could be "scary" for a child, so perhaps a parent pre-empting this through a discussion with the child may be appropriate. However, to avoid the impression of an alliance with one parent or the parent inadvertently miscommunicating the nature of the process to the child, any parental explanation should always be followed up by a letter from the mediator.

Age

Article 12 extends the right to express a view to all children 'capable of forming' a views on matters affecting them. Lundy et al (2019: 402) argue that assessing a child's capacity to form a view and how that view is expressed must not be determined through an adult-centric prism. Children need only to be capable of forming a view. They are not required to demonstrate the competency of an adult. General Comment No. 12 discourages State Parties from placing an age on competency. Instead, they should '*presume* that a child has the capacity to form their own views and recognise that they have the right to express them' (UNCRC General Comment No. 12, 2009: para 20, emphasis added). It goes on to acknowledge that even very young children can demonstrate understanding, choices and preferences through play, body language, facial expressions, drawing and painting. Once elicited, the weight to be put on the child's views will be assessed considering the child's age and understanding.

Like their counterparts from the focus groups (see Chapter Two), the young people who had experienced CIM advocated for flexibility over the age at which young people should be allowed to be heard. Younger interviewees could envisage children younger than them benefiting from the process. While a teenage interviewee had some concerns that very young children might find it difficult to grasp the situation or to talk to a stranger, one interviewee who said they were "6 or 7" when they met the mediator thought that the opportunity to meet a third party could help children to open up about issues that they were not comfortable discussing with their parents. They thought that children aged "5 or 6" should have the opportunity to benefit from CIM. Reflecting the views of others, Greg thought that provided the CIM was conducted well, and the child was not pressured to decide, children as young as his sibling (who was under nine when they spoke to the mediator) can benefit from CIM because the process brings clarity, helps the child to gauge what is going on and gives them a helpful outlet in which to talk about their parents' relationship. Carrie thought a universal offer was needed to ensure fairness and equality of treatment nationwide.

The setting: face-to-face and remote mediation

Twelve of the 20 young people had seen the mediator face-to-face, usually at the mediator's office but sometimes at school. While a few relationship professionals had questioned whether school was an appropriate setting for CIM meetings, the young people who had met the mediator in school had no issues. Alfie told us that it "did definitely help a lot going to [my] school ... [as] it was an area that I would spend six hours a day navigating through ... and I just knew [it]. ... So, it just felt a lot more comfortable."

Six young people had met the mediator remotely via Microsoft Teams/Zoom or equivalent, and one by telephone. This included one who had spoken to the mediator via Zoom and the telephone, who preferred Zoom since it was easier to read emotions and pick up on "cues" when you could see someone's face. As interviews took place between February 2020 and March 2021, those who had met the mediator remotely only did so of necessity due to the COVID-19 pandemic. However, for each, it had been a positive experience. Jake said it had lessened any sense of anticipation in the run-up to the meeting. Carrie thought she would have been more nervous about meeting someone face-to-face than remotely. Jonny liked that he could see his younger siblings more directly on a Zoom call than in an office environment and could "see how they felt".

Several young people who had face-to-face mediation spoke about the ambience and facilities of the room. Young people valued the mediator's efforts to put them at their ease. Several mentioned the quality of the biscuits, and these small gestures should not be underestimated. Toys for younger children, whiteboards, drawing materials and books were all welcomed, as were homely touches. Daisy liked that there was "a bookcase with lots of books in and like just little things you would find around like your house and stuff, so that actually made me feel a bit more like at home". The ambience helped young people be open with the mediator. Blake told us, "I liked going there because it was nice and calm, and you feel that you can just tell [the mediator] all about it, and they would understand." Parents also appreciated the mediator's care in creating a soothing ambience for their child. They disclosed how the mediator had carefully thought through the pre-meeting contact with the child, how they would greet the child, the room's setup, and the availability of age-appropriate toys and drawing materials.

Careful thought must be given to the backdrop and circumstances when mediating online so that young people feel similarly at ease. Mediators must ensure that the child concerned is not hungry or thirsty and has a safe, confidential place to conduct the online CIM. Provided the meeting was carefully planned, there was nothing from our evidence to suggest that CIM could not work well online. While an online format was chosen out of necessity, some children indicated that this had facilitated their voices being heard more readily than a face-to-face session would have.

The format

When there was more than one sibling, practice varied regarding whether sibling groups were seen together or apart.

The FMC Code of Practice (2018: para 7) requires that at least part of the Mediation and Information Assessment Meeting must include an individual element with each participant to allow the mediator to undertake domestic abuse screening. We suggest that best practice in CIM should be to offer each child a one-to-one with the mediator before any joint session with their siblings. Freddy could not recall being offered an individual meeting, but instead, "it was suggested we do it together, and we were absolutely fine with that, so we just went ahead with it". His siblings confirmed that the discussion of whether to have a separate meeting took place with all siblings present and that they had agreed unanimously to a joint session. The issue with that approach, just as with joint Mediation and Information Assessment Meetings, is that a child may not feel able to request a separate meeting when the invitation is put to the sibling group together.

An individual element to CIM, when there is a sibling group, would allow a child to express a contrary view to their sibling(s) or discuss matters that they would feel uncomfortable raising in the presence of their sibling(s). This is particularly relevant where there are issues of coercive control. Alfie's younger sibling disclosed being afraid of one parent. The mediation session was conducted partly together (which Alfie thought had helped his sibling to be more confident in the session) and partly separately. In the joint meeting, he and his sibling had been able to discuss things they "had in common that we both knew each other had suffered" and then their respective "big private stuff" in their one-to-one session, which he preferred "because there was some stuff that I did not want my [sibling] to hear that I thought might have upset [them] quite a lot".

As noted elsewhere, several eldest siblings appeared to take on a protective responsibility towards their younger siblings (Kay-Flowers, 2019: 138). Younger siblings valued this support. Molly, who said she was six or seven years old when she met the mediator, told us, "I didn't really know what was going on and [sibling] was a bit older than me. So, it was quite nice to have [sibling] next to me." Mediators must be flexible about the CIM format to make it as easy as possible for the child. Nevertheless, to uphold a child's right to an opportunity to express a view ('space') and have the expression of their views facilitated appropriately ('voice') (Lundy, 2007: 933), an offer of a meeting separate from their siblings should be made to the child individually.

The meeting

Before considering young people's satisfaction with the process of CIM, we reflect on how the CIM meeting, as explained to us by the young people, measured against the FMC Standards (FMC, 2014). Standard 6.4(j), for example, requires that '[m]ediators should offer and arrange ongoing support and further meetings with the child or young person as appropriate, as CIM is a process, rather than a one-off meeting'. Most children (17 of 20) disclosed having met the mediator only once. One sibling group had had ongoing telephone support. In another family, which involved one parent's thorny mental health issues, the child saw the mediator three times. Otherwise, the young people saw the mediator only once. However, the mediator had reassured several that they could return if needed. One child, for example, disclosed that her sibling had been reassured that she could return if she were worried about the transition to secondary school. The young people recognized that others might feel reticent to express their feelings in a one-off meeting. They may need several meetings with the mediator to be comfortable enough to express their views.

Regarding the meeting, most mediators (14 of 20) tended to see the children themselves, sometimes out of necessity, as they were sole practitioners. Those whose practice was that the child saw a different mediator (or child consultant) to the parents did so either because of confidence issues or because they felt strongly that this was a better model. Stephanie

Upton preferred this model because she thought "it's much more powerful to have a different voice giving feedback … rather than somebody who is trying to hold two perspectives". David Leighton thought it ensured that "the children's views can be contained, and the mediator isn't touched by stuff that isn't helpful to feed into the mediation process". However, primarily, the reason given by the mediators who preferred this model was because, as Briony Simpson told us, it avoided the risk of the mediator losing their impartiality, or at least the perception of loss of impartiality by one or both parents. Three-quarters of the parents (N=9) saw the same mediator as their child. They appeared to simply go along with whatever process was offered to them. No parent disclosed a preferred model save for Mark Bell, who said, "If they had seen a different mediator, I would have been scratching my head a bit because I would have said, 'Well, that doesn't make a lot of sense to me' as you need the same person, [you] have to hear the same story." The children may not have known whether they saw the same mediator as their parents, so we did not ask them this question.

The feedback session

In the focus groups, Aleah underscored the importance of the child and the mediator agreeing precisely what would be "fed forward" to the parents because "in some cases that's the first time the young person has spoken to anyone about how they feel and … a lot of emotion comes out that you might not want both parents to hear". As outlined later in 'Satisfaction with the process', the children, and most of the parents, were satisfied with how the child's views had been fed back to the parents.

The risks of child-inclusive mediation

As discussed in Chapters Two and Three, the focus group participants, relationship professionals and mediators expressed three concerns about hearing directly from children: it might be daunting for the young person involved and may place them under too much pressure; parents might try to manipulate the young person, or they may not listen to the child's expressed views. Here, we consider these three risks as discussed by the young people who have experienced CIM (also drawing on the parents' opinions where relevant). We also consider the risks associated with parents hearing unpalatable messages from the mediator's feedback following the meeting with the child. The young people and parents acknowledged the potential risks, although most stressed that this was not their experience. Broadly, the young people and parents believed that any risks identified could be mitigated partly by ensuring that only experienced, talented mediators undertook CIM.

Pressure

While this had not been their experience, the young people who had experienced CIM recognized the risk that a child, especially younger children, might feel pressured. Daisy said, "When I went, like I was nine or ten, so I didn't feel any pressure of it [*sic*], I just felt like I could be myself to [the mediator], where if you are a bit younger, you might not feel like that." As outlined earlier, Daisy's mediator had worked hard to ensure that the layout and homely contents of the room had created an ambience that relaxed Daisy.

Harry felt that a young person whose parents are separating might feel under pressure, whether the parents attended mediation or not. Still, the mediator's careful framing of feedback to the parents to reduce the risk of hurt feelings, and the child's ability to determine what is fed back to each parent, can relieve the risk of the child feeling pressured. Carrie felt that the parents and the mediator carefully explaining the process to the child before the child meets the mediator would help reduce any pressure the child may feel. Participation must be optional so that those who might find the process pressurizing can decline an invitation to participate.

Six parents were concerned that a child might feel under pressure, particularly to "choose" between their parents. Again, the parents emphasized the mediator's skill, with the mediator creating an ambience whereby the child did not feel pressured and carefully managing the expectations of both parents and children to avoid this risk.

Manipulation

Some young people interviewed thought there was a risk that a parent might manipulate a child or use the process strategically "as a tool" (Anna) to bolster their case, in which case the child's answers may not reflect their genuinely held views.

Careful screening of the parents for suitability before mediation, the child having the choice to decline an invitation to CIM, and the skills and training of the mediator were all highlighted by the young people as essential to guard against such manipulation.

Reflecting international research (Parkinson and Cashmore, 2008: 82), several parents were equally concerned that the child might be manipulated by the other parent (or, in one case, the resident grandparent). Trevor Cox had been initially "dead against" CIM for this reason, but the skills of and careful preparation by the mediator persuaded him to engage in the process. One mother disclosed that the father had insisted on taking the children to the CIM session and had told them on the journey that children with the contact regime for which they had expressed a preference "were proven to be unhappier" than children with the routine favoured by the father. However carefully the mediator has screened and prepared the parents for CIM, manipulation of this nature remains a risk. As with the young people, parents highlighted the mediator's skill and experience to guard against manipulation and identify if it had happened in a case.

Parents not listening

As with their peers and the adults, young people who had experienced CIM recognized the risk that parents may not heed the child's expressed view. However, they tended to be pragmatic about this. Harry highlighted that this was "a risk with or without mediation because obviously an adult can just ignore [the child] and say that a child's opinion doesn't matter, but at least with mediation, there is another adult who understands the child and is able to sort of convey their message to the parents". Jonny thought that even if the parents discounted the child's views, there was a benefit in the parents at least knowing what those views are.

All but two siblings reported that their parents had listened to and taken account of the child's views when fed back to parents, although the young people recognized the risk that other parents may not do so. Ellie's mediator had given her the option of getting back in touch if the parents were not sticking to the agreement so that the mediator could speak to the parents. Ellie credited this with ensuring that her parents complied with the arrangement. For some parents, this 'open-door' policy may suffice. However, it puts the onus on the child to be proactive in requesting further CIM either via a parent or by contacting the mediator directly. It may lead to disappointment if the parents choose not to re-engage at that stage. The child's interests may better be protected by an agreement with the parents and the child for the mediator to check back with the child at an agreed future date that the arrangement still works satisfactorily. This would prevent young people from being locked into an arrangement made in CIM that no longer works for them or may have become unsafe (Family Solutions Group, 2020: 96).

Two mothers (as discussed in Chapter Five) were happy with the process of CIM but not the outcome because, as they had expected, their ex-partners had not listened to and acted upon the children's views. While not their personal experience, several others raised parents not listening to their child's views as a potential risk.

Unpalatable feedback

A further risk raised by a minority of parents and some young people was that parents might hear messages from their children via the mediator that would be hard for them to take. The young people spoke of repercussions within the family from the parent(s) hurt by the message. Both young people and parents thought that the mediator reframing the message could take some of the sting from difficult feedback.

Ultimately, young people and parents underscored the need for highly skilled mediators to conduct CIM to manage identified risks. As discussed later, the young people and parents were highly satisfied with the mediator's skills, and the process.

Satisfaction with the process

Overwhelmingly, young people and their parents were satisfied with the process of CIM; even the minority of parents and young people who were dissatisfied with the outcome (see Chapter Five). Some parents were less satisfied with the mediation process than with the child-inclusive element.

What children liked about the process of child-inclusive mediation: 'audience'

Reflecting the views of some of the practitioners and parents on the purpose of CIM as primarily a means to progress to a decision, some young people were pragmatic and liked that CIM "got things sorted" (Alex). However, most young people spoke of mental health and wellbeing benefits that went far beyond making progress. As the relationship professionals had indicated, the young people who had experienced CIM reported that it informs, reassures and respects the child. In short, they felt listened to ('audience', Lundy, 2007: 933), and this had led, in many cases, to improved relationships between the young people and their parents, as discussed further in Chapter Five. In addition, those who had experienced CIM appreciated its future focus, and the ability to filter messages through the mediator and have the mediator reframe the message so that the parents were more likely to listen ('audience') and act upon what they have heard ('influence').

In Lundy's model, the third requirement is a 'right of audience', which Lundy defines as 'a *guaranteed* opportunity to communicate views to an identifiable individual or body with the responsibility to listen' (Lundy, 2007: 937, emphasis added). The evidence from the focus groups with young people and practitioners (see Chapter Three) is that this opportunity is far from *guaranteed*. Yet, the evidence from the young people who had been afforded such an opportunity was that when they felt that an experienced professional had listened to them and relayed their wishes to their parents sensitively, this had been therapeutic.

Informing the child

Research has shown that when parents separate, young people want to be informed about what is happening and that parents withholding information to protect their children from additional worry or upset, compounds their children's confusion and uncertainty about the future (Butler et al, 2002: 92). Staying informed is comforting for young people, providing assurance about the path ahead at a time of uncertainty and upheaval in their lives (Carson et al, 2018: 42). Informing children is therefore not a 'one-off' event. Children need ongoing information as family circumstances change (Murch, 2018: 58). In Lundy's model (Lundy, 2007: 933), a child's right to space and a voice is inextricably linked to their article 13 right to information, article 5 right to guidance from adults and article 19 right to protection from harm. The consensus from the young people who had experienced CIM was that they welcomed and found helpful the mediator's explanations about the CIM process (and the legal process of separation more generally) given before and during the CIM meeting. Several young people described their mediator as 'approachable'.

In interview, George, whose parents did not mediate until some years after the separation, reflected that it would have helped him had it come earlier in the process as it would have given him a better understanding of what was happening. In contrast, Chloe, who was only six or seven when she met the mediator not long after her parents separated, indicated that she liked seeing her "friendly" mediator to talk about "things that ... I was worried about or didn't know about. It just made me feel a bit more aware of what was going on". She felt that CIM could similarly help other children if they were worried about something but did not want to tell their parents, knowing that the mediator "will keep it a secret if they want it a secret, or not a secret if they don't want it a secret". She thought this might be particularly beneficial to only children or eldest siblings (like her) who did not have an older sibling with whom to discuss their concerns. Feeling better informed helped to ease young people's anxieties.

CIM also helped young people better understand their parents' and siblings' preferred contact regime. Jonny felt that the information they had received had "benefited" him and his younger siblings in clarifying a previously unclear situation, which "was nice to have some sort of base to then go off". He concluded that CIM gives young people confidence and a better understanding of what will happen. Alfie also thought that it had helped him and his younger sibling to "get a whole gauge of what's going on and how everything is working on paper, so it wasn't just like we had overheard arguments about stuff, and it was more like we actually knew like what the plan was". He thought CIM would help other young people in his situation to bring "clarity to the kids". The young people confirmed what the relationship professionals believed to be the case; giving young people an outlet to be better informed about the process (and helping them process their grief) can hugely benefit their psychological wellbeing and recovery.

Reassuring the child

Children whose views are sought report feeling reassured (Bell et al, 2013: 139; Kay-Flowers, 2019). Our findings chime with this finding. Many of the young people interviewed, as Anna explained, "felt really reassured" after meeting the mediator. The mediator helped Anna reframe her parents' separation so that "rather than it being something really kind of big in my life and scary that felt insolvable, I feel like [the mediator] offered hope that kind of things would get better". The mediator's experience proved reassuring for the young people. Greg, who said he was "100 per cent satisfied" with the mediation process, told us that the mediator made him and his sibling "feel very comfortable, and it felt like [the mediator] had lots of experience, so she kind of knew what I was going through". Daisy appreciated speaking to an independent, empathetic person who understood her position: "Sometimes when you talk to other people … it's quite hard to talk to them because they haven't been through the things that you have been through, whereas I felt like [the mediator] knew the position I was in with it all."

Acknowledging that the separation was difficult for their parents and that it can be hard to talk to them at this time, young people prized having an independent ally who was "there for them". As Ellie put it, "It gives [children] a chance to say what they want [and] … gives them kind of a sense that somebody is there for them."

Several young people spoke about the physical release of tension they experienced, having communicated with the mediator; Alfie, Alex and Andrew all spoke of stress lifted from their chests. Alex, who said that he had "enjoyed every single bit" of the process, said that it had "taken so much off my chest, and it really has helped me, mentally and physically". Ellie felt that allowing her to be included and have a say in the decision-making had made her "feel better about the whole thing". Carrie disclosed, "Once I said all of that [to the mediator], it feels like it's all off my shoulders and I don't have to worry about it anymore." Therefore, her advice to young people considering mediation was to accept the offer because "[it gets] all of that out of your mind then you don't worry about it anymore". Similarly, Daisy had found it therapeutic to offload to the mediator: "I liked it because I could tell her what I felt about the whole thing and wouldn't have to think about [it]." Several mediators confirmed feedback from parents that their child had also spoken of the weight lifted from their shoulders following the session with the mediator.

CIM helped Christina, as the mediator normalized and validated some of her feelings while giving her the confidence to state her wishes clearly and appreciate that (given her age and maturity) she had a right to be heard in the decision-making. Carrie said that it would have felt "weird" to speak to her friends about her parents' separation and that she appreciated the chance to talk to someone "older" about how she felt, which made "the situation a lot less scary and more happy and joyful than just like waiting and not talking to anyone and then just becoming more upset and upset about it".

Reflecting the female bias in the mediation profession, 13 of the 20 young people interviewed had seen a female mediator. Girls who had seen a female mediator were more likely to stress the emotional support they had received from the mediator. Some boys, like Alex, were more pragmatic, appreciating the progress made in CIM. However, the boys undoubtedly found the process reassuring. George felt it had been a helpful forum to "let [his] emotions out". Richard (who had seen a male mediator) reflected that he had been trying to block out his emotions and avoid engaging with his parents' attempts to discuss the separation with him, but CIM "forces you to think about it and make new opinions and talk to a professional about the situation". He described mediation as a "spark" to help you think about options. Blake appreciated the mediator's understanding and reassurance that things would get better. The tendency for boys to stress the benefits of weight lifted from their chest (mentioned earlier) may reflect a tendency among boys to internalize how they are feeling. Speaking to the mediator might engender more discomfort in boys than girls, even though boys appreciated that it had helped them.

These findings add to a growing body of evidence that hearing from children when parents separate can lessen children's anxieties (see Barlow and Ewing, 2020: 37).

Respecting the child

Neale and Flowerdew (2007: 27) have argued that when parents separate, the need for recognition, respect and participation are as crucial to children's wellbeing as their need for care and protection. Recognition and acknowledgement that it is their lives that will be affected has been cited as the main reason why children wish to participate (Parkinson and Cashmore, 2008: 67). Failure to consider young people's views can make them feel that their wishes do not matter to their parents (Kay-Flowers, 2019: 150). While unaware of their article 12 rights, many of the young people interviewed appreciated being given a voice and, more importantly, feeling heard. Freddy liked "the idea that my parents cared about my opinion". Harry told us that CIM had helped make clear what he and his siblings wanted, and without CIM, "there's a probability that there'll be kids of people going through divorce with their voices … lost". Harry thought that having a professional trained to speak to children and elicit their views allows them to be obtained without bias.

As Anna summed up, even if the outcome, ultimately, is not what they would have chosen, the process gives young people,

'A voice and they are being respected, even if the proceedings didn't go their way, they would know that somebody had heard them and, you know, there was a reason things had gone a certain way, and I also feel like it's actually quite cathartic for children to be able to kind of explain what's going on to someone and someone to listen to them.'

Protecting the child

The Harm Report (MoJ, 2020: 60) points out that, evidentially, listening more carefully to children can assist since it may give a better understanding of whether allegations of alienation have any merit. Only one child in interview disclosed feeling afraid of a parent but said that being able to tell a third party her true feelings had helped. As she put it:

> 'If I'm being honest, I'm scared of my dad. I told [the mediator] that and she tried to sort it out and she did make me feel more comfortable. ... I was scared that like if I said something to my dad ... he would think it's all my mum's fault that I am saying all that, which it isn't because I really do think that, and to say it to another person and know they won't go back to him just really made me a lot more happier of [sic] the situation.'

The outcome for this child was that she was not having direct contact with her father at this time, per her wishes, as explained further in Chapter Five. One other child disclosed that his father had a "coercive personality". Because of this, it had been easier to explain his feelings to the mediator rather than his parents directly.

Future focus

Mediation is a future-focused process (Roberts, 2014: 21). Carrie neatly summed up how this had helped her in the context of CIM:

'So, when I said something about what happened, she didn't really get her nose into a lot of it and say, "Oh, well, how did it start?" and all of it. She just said, "Oh, we can maybe do this", and then afterwards, she was just really nice, and she made me feel a lot more comfortable about the situation.'

Filtering and reframing

Two allied benefits of hearing from children raised by young people who had experienced CIM but not the relationship professionals were filtering and reframing. That is the ability to filter, via a third party, messages that the young people realized might be hurtful for their parents to hear or challenging for the young person to say, coupled with the mediator's skills in reframing those messages in such a way as to be more palatable to the parents. For several young people, the ability to filter messages to their parents via the mediator enabled them to be honest. As Jonny put it:

'There is less sort of emotion or like wanting to appease people when it's like a third party because it's someone different who I don't have a connection to. So, with Mum or Dad, I want to make them both like happy or whatever, so I change my own opinions, but this way, I knew if I wasn't personally telling them, then I could actually say what I meant.'

The boys interviewed particularly appreciated the ability to filter a message via the mediator. Filtering his preferred contact regime via the mediator helped Nathan feel less like he favoured one parent. He was thankful that the mediator delivering the message to his parents saved him from doing so. Freddy thought that having a professional third party involved had helped all family members keep track of the various options, and the mediator had been able to "relay the information more clearly" than if Freddy had been directly discussing matters with his parents. As Richard reflected, filtering the message through the mediator meant that his parents had not judged the children. It was also helpful for him because "sometimes it's a bit hard to say exactly what you think … and you sort of need someone to carry the message".

Just as the ability to filter the message helped young people to be honest about how they felt, they thought that their parent hearing the views from a mediator was more powerful and more likely to be accepted as the child's honest opinion than had the children said it directly. Alex thought his parents might not accept the veracity of his views if he spoke to them directly, but having heard it from the mediator, "they know that it is true". Others thought that talking to the mediator brought clarity. Freddy thought the mediator could "relay the information more clearly" than if heard directly.

The mediator's ability to reframe messages to take the sting from the child's views was appreciated. Harry recognized that some of his feedback might be hurtful for his parents to hear, so he was grateful that the mediator "definitely putting it in more, you know, gentle ways would be a lot easier" for his parents. Nathan liked "being able to tell the mediator [who] would sort of tell [his parents] in sort of a more … well basically where I didn't have to do it". As the eldest sibling, Christina chose to relay how she felt about the contact arrangements to her father directly. Nevertheless, she appreciated the mediator's expertise in helping her to put that message across in "a kinder way" so that her father would not feel that she was angry with him.

In cases involving coercive control or mental health difficulties, the 'buffer' of a third party was particularly appreciated. One teenage boy described his father as coercive, a young girl indicated she was frightened of hers, and a third young person disclosed that one of her parents had mental health problems, making it difficult to get her point across. Reflecting similar comments from other young people with complicated relationships with one parent, one young person concluded that filtering her message through the mediator had "definitely got the point across" to her parent with mental health issues better than she could by explaining how she felt directly. Stringent screening processes for suitability for non-court processes are a must. Domestic abuse and mental health issues may be contraindications if they impede parties' ability to advocate for their interests (Barlow et al, 2017b). However, the evidence from the young people who disclosed such issues as features of their parents' separation was that CIM had been helpful.

What children did not like about the process of child-inclusive mediation

There was very little that young people disclosed that they did not like about the process of CIM. One young person expressed concerns about the cost implications for families less affluent than his own. Even the minority of young people who were unhappy with the outcome or whose parents withdrew from the process were generally positive about their experiences of the process. One parent withdrew from the process due to mental health issues. Nevertheless, their child had found her time with the mediator to be "uplifting" and "a positive thing". Claire, who (as discussed in Chapter Five) was unhappy with the outcome, was more ambivalent: "The lady was quite nice, she was quite normal, like not weird, and we got biscuits ... I wasn't bothered about the whole thing." Jemima, who was also disgruntled at the outcome, thought that the process was "okay". She reflected that even though it did not work for her parents, it could be a good process for other young people because it would help them to understand the situation better.

Communication

The one recurring disappointment many young people voiced was that CIM had little effect on their parents' ability to communicate with each other. As outlined in Chapter Five, reaching an agreement in CIM, as most parents did, had stopped arguments about child arrangements. However, several young people did not think there had been a noticeable lasting improvement in their parents' relationship. Anna said that her parents' communication in the mediation process had improved but that the ongoing court proceedings had meant that this had not been sustained. Daisy thought that mediation had not helped her parents' ongoing relationship, although it had helped them reach an agreement without arguing. Joel concluded that while the CIM had helped his parents get a child-led outcome, it had raised other "child management" issues that had led to ongoing disagreements between his parents. Claire reflected that getting both parents to agree to the children being heard had led to more arguments between them. Alfie thought any improvement in his parents' relationship because of CIM was short-lived.

What parents liked about the process of child-inclusive mediation

Just as their reasons for choosing CIM tended to be both parent-focused and child-focused (see Chapter Three), what parents liked about the process of CIM fell into these two categories. Parents liked that it helped them make child-led progress and reassured them that their children were coping with the separation. Parents also appreciated many things about the process described by the young people, such as reassuring and respecting the child and, where necessary, protecting the child (and parent). For some, engaging in the process improved family relationships, which we discuss further in Chapter Five.

Reaching child-led agreements

We discuss which families resolved matters in CIM and satisfaction with outcomes in Chapter Five, highlighting that parents appreciated the child-led agreements reached. They were grateful that the process itself had ensured that the child's voice was at the centre of the decision-making. Tanya Adams commented that engaging in CIM ensured she and her ex-partner had had a "very child-centred separation", which she described as "liberating". She explained, "When the children are at the centre ... it makes it easier because they are the focus, and if they are the focus, and you both love them, it actually gives you the answers."

Reassuring the parent

As well as reassuring the child, CIM reassured parents that the children were coping. Rose Enstone "particularly liked" that it gave "independent feedback" on how her children had coped with the separation. She disclosed that "to hear from an independent person how happy and relatively untainted by it all they are, that was really heart-warming and quite a relief".

For Felicity Ingham, "it was a huge support ... to feel that [her children] have got someone else who has got their back" and gave them an impartial space in which to speak. Bobby Gordon thought that it had been "reassuring [and] reaffirming" that matters would proceed "at the pace of the children" as he had hoped.

Reassuring the child

Brown and Campbell (2013: 195) found that parents whose children met with a mediator reported that their children felt reassured by the opportunity to express themselves to a neutral and informed professional. Similarly, the parents we spoke to, particularly the mothers, appreciated the mediator's emotional support to their children and felt that it had had a therapeutic benefit. Felicity Ingham indicated that it was essential to recognize that the children and the adults might need "support from a third party". Melinda Kingsley said that her eldest child found the acknowledgement in mediation that "it was okay to have feelings" had "made them feel so much better about everything". Wendy Lund reflected that providing an independent outlet "has probably taken quite a load off" her child, who was naturally a worrier and found it hard to express feelings.

Respecting the child

Stalford et al (2017: 211) suggest that if young people are to develop their legal literacy and realize their rights in practice, they require 'foundational rights-based information', that is, they need to know their rights; that they have the right to be heard and that their views should be given due weight.

Several parents appreciated that CIM had helped their child understand their rights, which was important because they did not know their child's rights. Tanya Adams felt that her children had felt "empowered" by the process and were "beginning to thrive" because they now understood that they "can drive their own lives through what has happened and that they are entitled to an opinion".

Filtering and reframing

Chiming with the findings of McIntosh and Long (2006: 8), and the young people, parents disclosed a greater readiness to listen to views that did not support their argument when these views came from their children and were conveyed empathically by an independent specialist. Several parents recognized that children could feel obliged to tell parents what they each want to hear, so they appreciated the independent professional through whom to filter their children's views, particularly if the child's message was unpalatable for one or both parents. Phil Jackson thought engaging in the process had alleviated some differences between him and his former partner and allayed some of their fears. Since they both wanted what was best for their children, hearing from them via the mediator gave a "much more honest perspective on the situation ... [because] it's really pretty defining what a child would say". Wendy Lund thought that her child had used mediation as a "crutch", a means by which the child could discuss her issues with her mother (Wendy) without getting "emotionally drawn through it all". More often, parents felt that it provided a valuable forum for the child to air grievances against the *other* parent, which the mediator could reframe and which the other parent was more likely to take heed of than if it had come directly from the child or the parent. Some, like Ellen Foxton, disclosed that while their parenting was inclusive of the child's voice, the process had helped the other parent to hear from the child. Melinda Kingsley thought that "the mediator listened to the children and probably worked with [ex-husband] to ... shape the situation into an acceptable level for everybody".

McIntosh and Long (2006: 8) report that parents, particularly fathers, described the feedback session as 'valued and transformative', and the parents in the present study made similar comments. As Bobby Gordon put it, "When you hear someone else expressing your children's wishes, it's like, 'Oh my God, why haven't we been listening to that?'" He described the process as "a reality check" for parents, adding, "When [the child's views are] said to you with someone else knowing what your children feel as well, it hits a nerve."

Trevor Cox appreciated working with an experienced professional who was able "to initiate that discussion and present it in a very constructive manner". Tanya Adams' conclusions reflected the views of several parents:

'The children have felt much safer and much happier because there is somebody else who is reframing [their views] and passing that message on and they felt comfortable enough to be able to say things about both of us actually to [the mediator] and then she would pass that message on.'

Some parents thought it helpful for children to hear messages from the mediator that the parent could not give them. Felicity Ingham said the father dictated the child arrangements to their teenage child. She wanted her child "to have someone that she could turn to who would give her a balanced view (that I couldn't do) and tell her that it wasn't right, because it's all very well me saying it's not right, but it needed to come from someone else".

Protecting the child

The Harm Report (MoJ, 2020: 75) outlines the deleterious impact of children's voices going unheard or muted in private law proceedings involving alleged domestic abuse. For parents who alleged that the other parent could be controlling or domineering, hearing from the child in CIM had afforded some protection for their children and, in the process, themselves. Doug Henderson hoped engaging in the process would provide "that extra layer of reinforcement that the children's safety needs to come first in terms of their relationship with their mum, and their views kind of concreted that". He felt that "pulling back the curtain" on the children's views in CIM had helped his children to articulate that they wanted to be safe, which enabled him to feel that he did not "need to carry the whole burden of their protection". Ellen Foxton said her children were scared to voice their opinions to their domineering father. CIM, she disclosed, "gave [the children] a voice, and I think also gave me and the [children] a bit of bravery, just like we wanted".

What parents did not like about the process of child-inclusive mediation

Overall, parents were satisfied with the process of CIM, even if dissatisfied with the outcome. Melinda Kingsley indicated she would give the process a "ten out of ten", although she was dissatisfied with the outcome. Similarly, though dissatisfied with the outcome, Mary Dobson felt that the process had been satisfactory. However, she was concerned that, as with her children, if a child's expressed views are not considered, it can be "more detrimental than not having a say". Some parents were disappointed that the process had not led to better communication between the parents, as discussed further in Chapter Five. The most frequently cited gripe was the cost of the process.

Power dynamics

Some parents were less satisfied with the mediation sessions than with the CIM element. Ellen Foxton, for example, was disappointed that while she had explained to the mediator how domineering her ex-husband could be, she had felt unable to get her view across adequately in the joint session. She had "hoped that [the mediator] could be a bit of a backup for me, but actually it was not really any different to just talking to someone normally". Admitting to listening in at the door of her children's remote CIM, she was disappointed that when the mediator fed back to the parents, he had "toned down" what the children had said negatively about their father and positively about her. She attributed this to the mediator understanding the "dynamic" between the parents but still felt short-changed by the feedback.

Costs

Despite strong support for the process of CIM, five parents raised that it is expensive. They felt that young people might benefit from a longer, more therapeutic intervention but that this might be prohibitively expensive. Some also expressed reservations about returning to CIM because of the cost implications.

Conclusion

From our analysis, there seems to be some way to go before Lundy's (2007) vision of article 12 compliant services for children are uniformly available. In Chapter Three, we showed that on the mediators' accounts, the FMC's requirement to ensure children aged over ten can express their views (FMC, 2018: 6.6.1) was not consistently applied. The young people we spoke to had had the opportunity to express a view ('space') and had been facilitated to express their views ('voice'). However, given the barriers to uptake identified in Chapter Three, and since the evidence presented in this chapter points to there being no consistent system for inviting them, there is a risk that others might not have been given these opportunities. In Chapter Six, we make recommendations to address these issues.

In Lundy's model, 'audience' requires that young people be assured the opportunity to express their views to an identifiable individual or body tasked with listening to those views (Lundy, 2007: 937). Overall, the evidence from this study is that this is still not the norm, let alone universal. The evidence outlined in this chapter points to mental health and wellbeing benefits for young people whose active participation in decision-making is facilitated ('voice') and their views listened to ('audience'). Young people feel informed, reassured and respected. Some felt better protected. They could express themselves more effectively (and their messages were more palatable) than if they had tried to communicate their wishes and feelings directly to their parents. It would suggest that CIM, when offered routinely to all children and young people capable of forming an opinion as anticipated by article 12 and facilitated by an empathetic, highly-skilled mediator, can be a "powerful tool" in enabling young people's right to be heard as "equal partner[s] in a family" as a mediator, Henry Sanderson, put it.

Reconceptualizing mediation to emphasize the relational element of autonomy within the family context would make it less likely that parents will feel pitted against each other in the mediation room, with the needs and voices of their children drowned out in the process. A relational approach acknowledges that, particularly within families, we are profoundly interconnected. It seeks solutions based on honouring relational responsibilities rather than a clash of individual rights and interests (Herring, 2017: 262). In CIM, a relational approach will help to counter the dominance of parents' autonomy of the traditional child-focused method, enabling young people to be heard as "equal partner[s] in a family". Our evidence shows that when parents take seriously their responsibility to listen to their children's wishes, and when young people's voices are facilitated in the process, the experience can be empowering, with benefits going far beyond simply helping their parents reach agreements. As discussed in the next chapter, their participation was also pivotal to the agreements reached.

FIVE

Outcomes of
Child-Inclusive Mediation

Introduction

This chapter sets out our findings regarding which families were able to resolve matters in child-inclusive mediation (CIM). It reflects on the extent to which the child's views had been acted upon and informed agreements reached about child arrangements to consider whether Lundy's fourth requirement of an article 12 compliant service for children whose parents separate, 'influence' (Lundy, 2007: 937), was met. Influence requires the child's views to be acted upon where appropriate. Where the process had taken place some time ago, it examines how well settlements had lasted from the perspective of the young people who had engaged in CIM (and parents). It further discusses, then compares, young people and parents' satisfaction with outcomes and the longer-term impact on the family and family relationships. For the minority dissatisfied with the outcome, it concludes by reflecting on what seemed to be driving their disappointment.

State Parties must ensure that all administrative decisions concerning children demonstrate that the child's best interests have been a primary consideration (UNCRC General Comment No. 14, 2013: para 14(b)). To demonstrate compliance, States must create the necessary conditions for children to express their points of view and ensure that their opinions are given due weight (UNCRC General Comment No. 14, 2013: paras 14(b) and 53). 'Administrative decisions' include decisions reached in mediation when parents separate (UNCRC General Comment No 12: para 32). In Chapter Three, we discussed the barriers to creating the necessary conditions for children to express their points of view when parents engage in mediation. In Chapter Four, for young people whose views were heard, we considered whether the processes in place facilitated or hindered their ability to express their views. In this chapter, from their perspectives and those of their parents, we will reflect on whether the views of young people who engaged in CIM were given proper consideration and due weight placed upon them per the child's age and maturity – in short, whether they had influence (Lundy, 2007: 937).

Resolving matters in child-inclusive mediation

As noted in Appendix I, the 12 parents and 20 young people interviewed came from 12 different families. Whereas Bell et al (2013: 136) reported that only just over a third of parents who engaged in CIM reached an agreement, in the present study, all but two families reached an agreement in mediation. Mediation broke down for one family where the child lived with the father because the mother, who had significant mental health issues, withdrew from the process and chose to cease contact with her child. Another family, in which the children lived primarily with the mother, had used CIM to support the children to process their feelings about the contact arrangements that had been in place for some years. The children chose not to have their wishes and feelings fed back to the parents, and the contact continued unaltered. In both cases, the child's primary home was unchanged following mediation. The remaining ten families had agreed child arrangements in mediation. In Table AI.1 in Appendix I we outline the pre-mediation child arrangements. The family in which the maternal grandparents had been primary carers moved to a shared care arrangement between the grandparents and the father (the mother was deceased). One primary mother arrangement moved to a shared care arrangement. Once both parents acquired their own homes, the family with a nesting arrangement agreed a shared care arrangement with the children staying slightly more with the mother. Otherwise, primary care of the child was unchanged following mediation. Agreements included visiting contact only for one child and no contact for another. The remaining agreements were for overnight contact. As mentioned later, the children's wishes had informed most agreements reached.

As detailed in Chapters Three and Four, the mediators and the parents are powerful gatekeepers to CIM. The mediators we interviewed did not extend an offer to participate to *all* children aged ten and over, despite the Code of Practice mandating this (FMC, 2018: 6.6.1). Two parents who agreed to CIM (Trevor Cox and Rose Enstone) indicated that the mediator had framed the offer positively, giving them the confidence to try, despite their initial reluctance. Had they instructed mediators less confident in their abilities as CIM mediators or the process, the outcome may have been different. Similarly, for children to be offered CIM, a confident mediator and two willing parents are required. Unsurprisingly, success rates are high when these factors coalesce. As Kirsty Oliver said: "[CIM] cases I have done are the ones where the parents have cooperated. They are prepared to allow their children to have a say, and as you would expect with parents like that, the outcomes are going to be better, because they are willing and open to that happening."

Reaching agreement: 'influence'

Respecting children's views can lead to better, more relevant and informed decisions regarding matters that affect them (Parkinson and Cashmore, 2008: 85; Lundy et al, 2019: 399). Children who indicate that they were consulted over or influenced the agreed child arrangements report higher degrees of satisfaction with the arrangements (Butler et al,

2002: 96; Parkinson and Cashmore, 2008: 75). From young people's perspectives, being 'listened to' is a two-way process that involves the relevant adults taking the time to hear and understand the young person's point of view and informing them about what is going on (Carson et al, 2018: 89). However, having given young people an opportunity to express a view and taken time to hear and understand that view, there must be mechanisms in place to ensure that the young person's view is taken seriously and acted upon as appropriate, in pursuance of their article 12(2) rights. The power of 'space', 'voice' and 'audience' are diminished unless they lead to 'influence'. Young people report that they would prefer that they are not asked for their views if their views are then not considered in the decision-making process (Barlow et al, 2017a: 18). Conversely, recognition of the right to have one's views taken seriously promotes a sense of self-esteem in young people (Lansdown, 2019: 5).

Children are vulnerable relative to adults, which justifies the special human rights the United Nations Convention on the Rights of the Child (UNCRC) accords them (Tobin, 2013: 396). Whereas constructing children as vulnerable and lacking capacity has traditionally been used to justify their need for protection rather than special rights (Guggenheim, 2007: 11), constructing children through a rights-based lens acknowledges their evolving capacities. It changes how they are viewed and the response to hearing from them. A vulnerabilities approach risks silencing children, but a rights-based approach requires that adults listen to children by actively seeking out their views and treating them seriously (Tobin, 2015: 169).

The right to participate does not mean that children will be the decision-makers. However, it does require that they contribute to the process (Parkinson and Cashmore, 2008: 63). Similarly, the right to have one's views taken seriously does not mean that the young person's views will always be acted upon. 'Influence', when properly implemented, does, however, require that the young person's views, once sought, are given proper consideration, weighted considering their age and maturity and that any decision made is reported back to them with an explanation of how and why the decision was reached (Lundy, 2007: 939; UNCRC General Comment No. 12, 2009: para 45; Lansdown, 2019: 9). We will measure the influence of the young people's views against this criterion.

Proper consideration

What, then, is meant by 'proper consideration' in the context of CIM? Our previous research has shown that when children's voices are not heard directly in mediation, then some mothers and fathers choose to invoke the child's 'best interests' as a means of justifying their preferred child arrangements regime (Smithson et al, 2015: 12). Hearing directly from the children in CIM should help to ensure that their views are given better consideration than when their views are heard in absentia. Proper consideration of children's views requires that adults be no longer the sole arbiters of the child's interests (Tobin, 2013: 431).

Attending to children's 'voice' requires that once obtained, children's views are taken seriously by those with the power to effect change in their lives (Hanna and Lundy, 2021: 468). Within the context of CIM, this is the parents, facilitated by the mediator. Having agreed to hear from their children in CIM, most parents had given their children's views proper consideration and come to agreements that reflected the child's wishes either entirely or the child's wishes had at least informed the decision reached. Wendy Lund and her ex-partner had, for example, reached quite complex arrangements involving time with stepsiblings and a parent and time with the parent alone based on their child's suggested contact regime.

Mark Bell said that depending on the child's level of maturity, they should be allowed to participate, and their views form part of the input into the decision-making. He likened the decision-making process when parents separate to a business environment:

'I am the [Leader], and I am being paid, and ultimately, it's my responsibility, but in order to reach a decision I have to sort of hoover up everybody's input. And then, take that back to the environment we are talking about, my [children]'s input is just as important as mine or my [ex-partner]'s because we are talking about them.'

"Hoovering up" the input of others but retaining ultimate responsibility for the decision might sound somewhat paternalistic. However, following CIM, Mark had agreed to the children's preferred contact regime even though their views coincided with their mother's rather than his. However, his reasoning, which he explained to the children, had not been that he had recognized their right to have their views taken seriously; instead, he had "taken the pragmatic decision to allow Mummy to have her way".

As discussed later, cases that ended without an agreement or a short-lived agreement tended to be because one or both parents did not adequately consider the children's views.

Due weight

As Lundy points out, it is necessary to consider the extent of influence, 'what constitutes the "due" in the "due weight"' to be placed upon the child's views (Lundy, 2007: 937). Tobin recognizes that since the weight to be placed on the child's views under article 12 is per their age and maturity, the adults concerned (here, the mediators and parents) may seek to use this to retain authority over the child effectively. However, he offers an alternative reading of article 12, which demands 'that adults cede their authority over children and actively facilitate their citizenship' (Tobin, 2013: 418). Tobin argues that parental rights and responsibilities remain subject to the child's evolving capacities and must be exercised 'to *guide and assist* the realisation of children's rights' (Tobin, 2013: 424, emphasis in original). Therefore, article 12 does more than allow a child to influence decision-making. It requires that the child's views *must* be given due weight, anticipating that the views of a child of sufficient maturity and understanding will be determinative (Tobin, 2013: 432). Children *must* be allowed to play an active role in decision-making, should they wish to do so, consistent with their evolving capacities (Tobin, 2013: 434; Dimopoulos, 2021: 440). Save in the most damaged of family relationships, when parents separate, children report that they wish to be treated as 'respected agents' along with their parents in the decision-making rather than having full agency (or indeed, responsibility) for making decisions (Parkinson and Cashmore, 2008: 64; Daly, 2018a: 37). The notion of evolving capacity, as conceptualized by Daly (2018a; 2018b), Dimopoulos (2022) and Tobin (2013; 2015), is a relational one in which, with direction and guidance from their parents, children are empowered to exercise their autonomy in the determination of their best interests, per their evolving capacities.

Where the families had reached lasting agreements (to be discussed later), the young people we spoke to felt their views had been given due weight. Several young people confirmed that the regime they suggested had 'definitely' been agreed upon in full; others that their views on what they liked (or did not like) had informed the decisions reached. Save as discussed later, all were happy that their views had been given due weight.

Nathan reported that having considered the pros and cons of each contact regime with the mediator and trialling his parents' respective preferred regime, they had come to "a combined family decision" that he and his siblings were happy with and which had continued successfully since reached just under 12 months earlier. Daisy said she and her sibling had told the mediator what they did not like about the current contact arrangement. Once the mediator had fed back the children's views, her parents had "made this whole plan so that mine and [sibling]'s thoughts and ideas were in there too". Freddy reflected that the agreement may not have been drastically different had the children's voices not been heard. Nevertheless, he appreciated that the children's views had been used to formulate the settlement. He said, "It was definitely good for our parents to see our opinion and use that to formulate a system which ultimately affects everyone."

The parents reported that the agreements reached had been either steered or determined by their children's input. Bobby Gordon reported that his children had not explicitly said when they wanted to spend time with each parent. However, the mediator had taken "pointers" from them, which the parents had considered to "steer" the agreement reached. He felt that even if the children had only contributed to "one or two per cent of the decision-making process ... in their eyes, they have done 98 per cent of [it] just by saying something". As a result, the children "feel at the forefront of the decision-making now, they feel like they have had a hand in it. They feel like they have arranged it". The child-led agreement had worked well for 12–18 months, and when the parents suggested a change for practical reasons, the children argued, "No, Daddy, we worked hard to get that. We want to keep that," and the parents had agreed that the arrangement would not be altered.

Where safety concerns had been raised, the parent's willingness to abide by the children's wishes was caveated with the need to keep them safe. Doug Henderson said that he had gone into the process fully prepared to "abide by" the children's wishes "within reason" and provided this did not compromise their safety. Others were prepared to take on board the children's wishes, but only if they mostly aligned with that parent's views. Phil Jackson said there was a threshold of contact with his child below which he would not have agreed to follow the child's wishes and would have "pushed for more" in that case. In the event, this was unnecessary as the child's views aligned with his.

Reporting back

While there was clear evidence that the young people's views had influenced the decisions reached, the young person's right to feedback on *how* their views had influenced the decisions was far from upheld. As outlined in Chapter Four, only two practitioners mentioned writing to the children after their meeting. No child disclosed having heard back directly from the mediator – 17 of the 20 young people reported meeting the mediator only once (with the remainder disclosing more than one meeting because of the need for ongoing support rather than for feedback purposes).

Did settlements last?

Research in Australia (McIntosh and Long, 2006; McIntosh et al, 2008: 113) and the United States (Rudd et al, 2015: 4) has shown that compared to child-focused mediation, CIM has been found to reduce re-litigation. In the present study, the threat of litigation was disclosed in only one case (another case was already in litigation when mediation commenced).

Of the 12 family groups, two did not reach an agreement in mediation. Of the remaining ten families, most agreements had been reached recently: two years before the interview (two), one year before the interview (one) and less than 12 months before the interview (seven). As most were recent, it was impossible to indicate whether agreements would be lasting. Since the interviews took place in 2021–1, most agreements were reached in the shadow of the COVID-19 restrictions. Save where these restrictions had made it challenging to implement agreements fully, the child-informed agreements reached were being followed in all but one family. This family engaged in CIM in 2018. The father quickly resiled from the child-led agreements reached. The children lived with the mother primarily. Having agreed that his teenage children could choose when to visit him, the father had reneged on this. He expected the children to visit per the pre-mediation contact arrangement. In a second family, an arrangement had been agreed upon in CIM based on the child's wishes, which was being followed. However, the mother indicated that the father was issuing court proceedings to seek more time with the child.

What children liked about the outcome of child-inclusive mediation: 'influence'

Of the ten families that had reached an agreement following CIM, the children of all but one family were satisfied with the outcome, mainly because their input had influenced the child arrangements agreed upon by the parents. Research shows that young people report being happy with the outcome of child arrangement decisions when they feel their voices have been heard and their views considered (Dunn and Deater-Deckard, 2001: 21; Smart, 2004: 487; Cashmore et al, 2010: 137). Our findings echo this: young people are satisfied with outcomes when they feel their views were acted upon ('influence', Lundy, 2007: 937) and, as discussed later, dissatisfied when they feel that their views were ignored.

Owning the outcome

When children are involved in the decision-making, they may generate proposals that the parents would not otherwise have thought of, making it easier for a parent to accept a solution without losing face (Al-Alosi, 2018: 18). Generating proposals that led to an agreement ensured that the young people felt that they 'owned the outcome' and as a result were highly satisfied. Alex was pleased that his involvement had led to an agreement, "It was quite helpful, the fact that it's been all sorted out now, because *I* did that." Jonny said that none of the proposals generated by his parents and discussed with the mediator had felt right to him, so he had formulated a proposal to which his parents had agreed wholesale. He was pleased that his parents were no longer in conflict over child arrangements because (with the support of his siblings) he "had made the decision for them".

Clarity

Several young people were more settled because, having been involved in the arrangement, there was greater clarity for them. Alex's parents separated several years before the mediation. He said the contact arrangement had been "all mixed over the place" before attending CIM. "It was just kind of like [going] to one parent's house without really any arrangements." He was pleased with the outcome and clarity, confirming that the agreement was based on his suggestions.

Linked to this, several young people had appreciated that their parents had taken on board their requests for fewer transitions or midweek disruptions. Whereas parents can sometimes become fixed on the quantity of contact (Barlow et al, 2017b: 177), save where safety concerns were raised, the priority for the young people was for good quality time with each parent, which worked practically for the young person and gave them a clear understanding of which home they would be spending time in throughout the week.

Improving family relationships

Child-inclusive approaches have been shown to improve parental relationships, which has a positive impact on children's emotional wellbeing post-separation (McIntosh and Long, 2006: 10; Walker and Lake-Carroll, 2014: 27). Overall, the young people were more optimistic than their parents about the outcome agreed having led to improved family relationships. Some young people spoke of improved relationships between their parents or themselves and their parents following CIM. Harry, for example, thought that it had helped his parents get on better, or at least "definitely no worse" because it had clarified what arrangements each parent and the children favoured. Jonny thought that before the mediation, his parents had been arguing as they were not entirely "taking time to understand each other at that point". The mediation had clarified what each parent wanted and the children's preferred outcomes, which, as well as resolving matters, had "helped get a sort of an openness between, I guess, all of us".

Ellie disclosed that CIM, in conjunction with joint counselling for her parents, had helped to improve their relationship, underscoring the need for a holistic approach to managing the adults' emotions on separation as advocated for by several relationship professionals. As outlined later in 'What children did not like about the outcome of child-inclusive mediation', several young people regretted that CIM had failed to improve communication between their parents.

Regarding the relationship between the parents and the child, Alfie felt the process had improved his communication with his parents. He reasoned that if he could be open with a stranger, he could be honest with his parents: "It opened me up a lot more and made me a lot more confident to speak to my [parents] about things, which just made a lot of stuff much, much easier and took a lot of stress off my chest." Another child thought the mediator had helped her see that she did not have to do anything she did not want to do. As a result, whereas before, she would agree to see her father even though she was afraid of him, she was now more open with her mother about feeling scared of her father. Reflecting research findings that CIM can improve father–child relationships (McIntosh and Long, 2006: 10; Walker and Lake-Carroll, 2014: 27), Joel reflected that once his father "had understood that I have an opinion and that I have one that maybe differs to his, then he [had become] more open to listening to it and understanding it". He thought that this extended to decisions beyond the child arrangements. Jonny thought hearing from the children had helped his father be more open with him and his siblings about the divorce, which he thought was positive. Greg considered that the CIM had been helpful to him as it had given him a forum to voice his problems with his parents to another adult. He felt things were "a lot clearer" between him and his parents because of the CIM and that it had helped his father understand why the agreed arrangement was in place and accept that it needed to revolve around the children.

When agreeing to speak to the mediator, one family group of siblings had done so on the basis that their views would not be fed back to their father as they had little confidence that he would take heed of those views. Unsurprisingly, while finding the discussions with the mediator helpful, the process had not impacted family communication.

Anna recognized that her father, who had primary care of her, had benefited from being able to get across how he felt about the situation. Improving parents' mental health is likely to make them more emotionally available to their children, which will benefit the child.

Safety

As outlined in Chapter Four, one child disclosed that the CIM had led to an arrangement whereby she did not have to see her father (of whom she said she was scared) unless she wanted to. She reported that the outcome had been empowering, "Now, after I have seen [the mediator], she made me feel like I don't have to do anything I don't want to. So, it's just made the situation a lot more better [sic] and less scary."

What children did not like about the outcome of child-inclusive mediation

Only two young people (siblings) expressed dissatisfaction with the outcome of CIM. These young people could distinguish their dissatisfaction with the outcome from their feelings about the process. As the younger child said, seeing the mediator "was okay, but it didn't really do anything". The elder child was annoyed that her parents had not taken her views "into perspective. ... Even though they have agreed on it, they are not doing it. They didn't really take it into play". She also thought that the meeting with the mediator had "backfired" for her younger sibling because, having expressed a view (to spend less time with the father), the father's dismissive response had been, "Well, you are too young, it's my say."

What parents liked about the outcome of child-inclusive mediation

As with the process, parents disclosed both child- and parent-focused reasons for what they liked about the outcomes reached in CIM. As they had hoped, hearing from the child helped them reach an agreement. Importantly for the parents, the agreements were child-led, resulting in wellbeing and developmental benefits for their children and more durable outcomes. The children had been empowered by the influence of their voices, equipping them to use their voices beyond the CIM setting. Some fathers reported that hearing the children's views had led to a more even playing field between the parents.

Child-led agreements

Our findings endorse earlier work on the value of child-inclusive processes. Respecting children's views can lead to better, more informed and developmentally sensitive agreements that the child finds acceptable regarding matters that affect them (McIntosh et al, 2008: 118; Parkinson and Cashmore, 2008: 68; Lundy et al, 2019: 399). Including the child's voice directly in the process makes it easier for parents to resist arrangements tailored to any sense of entitlement (McIntosh and Long, 2006: 9; McIntosh et al, 2008: 118). Parents who agree to their children being involved believe it can lead to better decisions and, therefore, to better outcomes and happier children (Parkinson and Cashmore, 2008: 85). The parents in our study reported that the child-led decisions reached had indeed resulted in their children being very happy with the outcome. Some, like Doug Henderson, were relieved that while they had come to CIM feeling "stuck" following feedback to the parents, "the children's voices were seen as definitive", leading swiftly to an agreement based on their wishes. Rose Enstone reflected the view of many parents that hearing from the children had led to a child-informed outcome that was "top-notch" and meant that the children were now in a "settled and stable and happy routine which suits everybody". Bobby Gordon thought that the mediator "deserved a medal" for managing to facilitate an agreement and help the parents avoid court. He said that both parents had had to compromise on what they wanted, but they had been prepared to do so as it had resulted in an agreement that "his children now love".

Fathers have described the feedback session about their children as valued and transformative (McIntosh and Long, 2006: 8). Again, there was support for this in the present sample. Doug Henderson described hearing his children's voices reflected in the mediator's feedback as "very emotional and kind of an eye-opener". Phil Jackson thought that hearing from children:

'Can bring quite a lot of clarity … I think if you … hear the words coming from your child, that this is something that they like or which they don't like, then you are going to pay a lot more attention to that than if it was coming from your ex-partner because their motivation may be to hurt you.'

Wellbeing benefits for the children

Several parents expressed regret that their children had been put through the trauma of parental separation. Therefore, their primary objective had been to minimize any fallout and reach agreements enabling their children to thrive. Tanya Adams said that she had felt personally "empowered" by the outcome reached but, more so, was relieved that the outcome had also been empowering for her children, helping to minimize the damage the separation had caused them, ensuring that they are "beginning to thrive". Likewise, Mark Bell said that his sole focus was that the children should retain their equilibrium and thrive (as he believed the agreement reached had achieved). Any outcome that achieved that aim and his children deemed successful would be acceptable to him. Even when the outcome was not what they had hoped, parents were satisfied, provided the outcome was what the children wanted. Wendy Lund explained that if her child was happy with the child-led agreement reached, "then that's what we are just going to have to go down the lines of, you know, put my thoughts and feelings to one side".

Developmental benefits

Some parents believe that involving their children in the decision-making on separation has empowering benefits that stretch beyond the immediate issue, helping them to develop life skills that improve the child's self-efficacy (Parkinson and Cashmore, 2008: 86). Several parents, including Mark Bell, echoed this sentiment. Whereas putting young people in "an interview type setting" can be uncomfortable for teenagers, they need to:

'[O]vercome that feeling and be able to make eye contact and listen to what is being asked of them and come up with a reply, and that's part of life, isn't it? So, it's part of kind of growing up process, you know, for a couple of hours your opinion is required here so, you know, you have to listen and give it, for your own benefit.'

Tanya Adams felt that her child was now more open to help-seeking. By voicing their opinions in CIM, she thought that her child had learned the importance of help-seeking, that there was no shame attached to it and that "it's part of life to get those things in place if you are going to thrive ... so it's set [child] up a bit there, you know, for the future and how to cope". Doug Henderson appreciated that while "empowered" might be "stretching it", his daughter "feels a lot more confident in that ... now she knows that her feelings and her ability to express her satisfaction or dissatisfaction [about] things will be taken seriously, and I think for a [age] child ... that's a big thing".

Improving family relationships

Brown and Campbell (2013: 195) found that parents whose children had participated in CIM reported having a greater understanding of the children's views. Bell et al (2013: 136) found that most parents who had engaged in CIM reported improved relationships with their children. However, they found that only just over a quarter disclosed improved inter-parental relationships, compared to almost 60 per cent of the control group of parents who had mediation that did not include the child. Parents in the present study reported a better understanding of their children's wishes, which improved family relationships – although primarily the parent–child relationship rather than the relationship between the parents. Melinda Kingsley thought that on marital breakdown, there is a tendency for each parent to want to be "right", so having the child's voice can help guard against parties becoming entrenched, which can help the family going forward. Tanya Adams believed that following CIM, her children could tell her what contact with their father they wanted, and she was now more receptive to their suggestions. In her view, it was also instrumental in improving their father's parenting. Bobby Gordon, who thought he had been in tune with his children's views before CIM, said that hearing their opinions in CIM had made him "even more in tune", resulting in the relationship between his children and between the children and each parent "blossoming". As outlined later, however, only two of the 12 parents reported any improvement in communication between parents, even less than Bell et al (2013: 136) reported.

Greater durability

Giving children a voice is associated with more durable agreements (McIntosh et al, 2008: 113; Walker and Lake-Carroll, 2014: 27). Several parents welcomed the opportunity for some external, professional verification of either the child's views or the agreement reached and credited this with ensuring the durability of the agreement. Mark Bell appreciated that the agreement reached came with a "sort of gold-plated badge on it saying that somebody else has approved this". He felt that the agreement was more likely to be durable since a mediator had facilitated it rather than it being the idea of one parent. When a further decision needed to be made, Bobby Gordon's children were adamant that if it led to arguments between their parents, then they wanted to go back to CIM, so the parents had agreed to listen, rationalizing that they would only hear the message via the mediator if they did not, "so even now it still plays a part in our relationship". However, as outlined, most agreements reached were recent and therefore whether they stand the test of time remains to be seen.

A level playing field for fathers

McIntosh et al (2008: 118) report that fathers feel that hearing from children produces a level playing field in circumstances where the primary carer mother was the de facto 'gatekeeper of the truth'. There was some support for this in our sample. Trevor Cox explained:

'The child mediator came in and said, "Right, this is what [child] has said", and there it was! I just sat back, and I was so relieved that ... what I had been fighting for all these years, I was right in what I was saying, because right up until that point I was still being told … [child] … doesn't want this … doesn't want that blah, blah, blah … ahh, the relief! I can't tell you how much relief I felt, you know, I call it a victory, but it wasn't just a victory for me, it was a victory for my [child].'

Doug Henderson also reported: "Every accusation, every claim, every wild thing that mum had said … as soon as the children's voices were heard, she retracted immediately, and she changed her tack in an astonishing volte-face."

What parents did not like about the outcome of child-inclusive mediation

As discussed later, only one parent was dissatisfied with the outcome of CIM. Otherwise, there was a correlation between whether parents resolved matters in CIM and satisfaction rates. The one major disappointment expressed was that although parents were satisfied with the outcome overall, there had been no perceived lasting improvement in communication between the parents.

Communication

Some parents expressed regret that the process had not improved communication between the parents as they had hoped. Ten of the 12 parents said that communication had not improved. Some had not expected an improvement in communication due to the ex-partner's mental health difficulties or controlling character or because the level of animosity was too great. Trevor Cox reflected this view, concluding that while he had hoped for better communication and improved working relationships across the two households, his "expectancy of [achieving] that would be minimal and certainly served to be the case since". Others hoped that communication between the parents would improve once a financial agreement was reached. Some reflected that it was a less destructive process than the alternative of court proceedings, and reaching an agreement meant there was less need for high levels of communication between the parents, reducing conflict. Some highlighted improving communication between the other parent and the children. For example, Ellen Foxton said involving the children in mediation had "unlocked a dialogue" between the father and the children, which meant they felt more able to state their views to him.

The two parents who said it had improved communication disclosed that they were now more mindful of the content of texts. However, one, Bobby Gordon, attributed this to work on communication in the mediation sessions rather than CIM. He credited the chance to talk, the ground the parents covered in mediation and the mediator's facilitation and skill at "extinguishing fires before they were even lit" in the main sessions as instrumental in effecting change. Even if parents had not experienced lasting improvements in communication, they appreciated the opportunity to be heard in the presence of a neutral third person. Phil Jackson was grateful that the joint mediation session had given both parents "space to speak ... space to express your views" and have those views reflected to them by the mediator so that each parent could judge whether they were being reasonable and rational. It should not be forgotten that the parents also need 'space', 'voice' and 'audience', which the mediation sessions can facilitate.

Cases unresolved in child-inclusive mediation: fringe benefits

In *Mapping*, we found that even if a case did not resolve in an out-of-court process, there were often fringe benefits of attempting the process, such as improved communication or a better understanding of the other's position (Barlow et al, 2017b). Saini (2019) found that knowing that their views were important to their parents and that their parents were trying to resolve matters amicably had benefited children who engaged in CIM, even if the case did not settle.

Of the young people we interviewed, only two cases involving four young people had not ended in an agreement between the parents regarding future child arrangements. In one of the cases, mediation was not attempted until several years after an arrangement had been put in place. The mother consulted the mediator because she felt the children needed an outlet to express their frustration at the father's lack of flexibility over arrangements that had been in place for some years. Even though the children chose not to have their views fed back to their father by the mediator, they found the process worthwhile. One sibling felt that speaking to the mediator had helped him understand the process and his father's position better and allowed him to "let my emotions out". Another had appreciated having someone independent from the family to talk to who understood the process and how they were feeling and could bring a different perspective and strategies for possible future issues. Even without any impact on the contact arrangement, the mother felt that the children had benefitted from the mediator's independent support.

In the other case, the child's mother had mental health difficulties and withdrew from the process (and from further contact). The child was saddened and reflected that the process had been difficult. However, in the absence of settlement, being open about how she had been feeling and her preferred outcome had helped her and her parents to "move forward from that point". It had helped to expose some of the issues in contact stemming from her mother's mental health problems and had helped her to come to terms with her parents' separation. Finally, it was helpful for her father to express how he felt about the family situation.

In two cases, agreement had been reached that either did not or may not last. In one case, while an agreement had been reached following CIM, the mother disclosed that the father had subsequently alleged that she had coached one of the children and that he intended to apply to the court alleging parental alienation. Nevertheless, the mother indicated that she felt that the outcome was positive in that the children had been able to say what they wanted to, which had given them confidence, and their feedback had validated what she had been saying. She indicated that the father had not listened, but she had not expected him to listen to or act upon the children's views, and her hypothesis had been proven.

The second case involved the family in which the parents and children reported dissatisfaction with the outcome. Neither the parent nor the children reported any fringe benefits of having engaged in the process, save the mother felt it had been helpful to her eldest child to hear from the mediator that her views could be decisive, given the child's age, and she could choose when she wished to see her father.

Parental dissatisfaction with outcomes

As indicated, the mother, who reported that the father had reneged on the agreement reached in CIM, was dissatisfied with the outcome. As Bell et al (2013: 137) found, her disappointment stemmed from her dashed hopes that hearing from the children would cause the father to change his behaviour. She also hoped that the process would stop the "petty arguments" around contact to establish a working relationship between the parents for the long term, but this, too, was unrealized. Like her children, she separated her feelings about the process from the outcome, indicating, "It wasn't that I didn't like [the process]. I just don't think it has solved any problems." The mother reported that the youngest child was becoming resentful of her father's attitude and was frustrated that having said what she wanted to in CIM, which her father acknowledged at the time, "none of it has changed", reflected similar frustrations of her children, as discussed earlier. Our findings support those of McIntosh and Long (2006: 9) and

McIntosh et al (2008: 120) that inclusion criteria for CIM should be *capacity-based*, that is, 'based on the ability of a parent to usefully participate in mediation and to consider alternate information'. The evidence from the mediators was that they would assess parental capacity as part of their assessment of the case's suitability for mediation. As Marjorie Jenkins put it, "What I am looking for is that degree of openness ... because I feel that I don't want to put a child in a situation where you are kind of bringing up false expectations of situations, and for a parent then to just dismiss what they have to say."

Conclusion

From our interview findings, most parents gave their children's views proper consideration in CIM, weighted considering their age and maturity. To that extent, Lundy's fourth requirement of an article 12 compliant service for children whose parents separate, 'influence' (Lundy, 2007: 937), had been met.

Parents had acted upon their children's views, and both parents and children reported having reached child-led outcomes with which they were satisfied, some delighted. Reaching child-led agreements brought wellbeing benefits for young people. They were proud to have contributed meaningfully to decision-making and influenced the outcome. They felt more settled as a result, and, from the perspective of many young people, it improved family relationships.

Even the minority of young people whose parents had not reached an agreement in CIM reported some fringe benefits (as confirmed by the parents) of engaging in the process. These included understanding the process better or appreciating an outlet to process emotions surrounding their parents' separation.

The parents and children who expressed dissatisfaction with the outcome did so precisely because the father had not taken seriously or acted upon the children's views. This highlights the need for a capacity-based assessment of parental suitability for

CIM (McIntosh and Long, 2006: 9; McIntosh et al, 2008: 120). That is not to say that the children should be denied an outlet (space) for expressing their views, as discussed in Chapter Six.

Influence, when properly implemented, requires that having acted upon the children's views, any decision made is reported back to them with an explanation of how and why the decision was reached (Lundy, 2007: 939; UNCRC General Comment No. 12, 2009: para 45; Lansdown, 2019: 9). The evidence indicated that this rarely happened, and we similarly suggest improvements in the following chapter.

SIX

Conclusions

Introduction

This book set out to consider what a study of experiences of child-inclusive mediation (CIM) can tell us about the call for a children's rights agenda to realize children's United Nations Convention on the Rights of the Child (UNCRC) rights when parents separate and make child arrangements out of court in England and Wales. In particular, it wanted to contribute a clearer focus on children's views and experiences, alongside those of parents and professionals, to this debate. Without the input of children's voices in research that underpins policy making, policy makers risk making assumptions about children's views, lives and needs that fail to reflect reality (British Academy, 2022: 40).

Our primary conclusion from our in-depth study is that there *are* compelling arguments for moving towards a family justice system that fully respects children's voices when parents separate in line with their article 12 rights. This is based first on the likely benefits to their mental health and wellbeing, given our findings in Chapters Two and Four, where we demonstrate consensus between the young people and relationship professionals on the importance of providing them with an outlet for their perspectives. Second, the clearly articulated views of young people themselves in those same chapters about the appropriateness of all children having more agency through a meaningful voice in arrangements affecting their lives, alongside their positive experiences of CIM, are compelling and confirm earlier research (Walker and Lake-Carroll, 2014; Barlow et al, 2017b; Carson et al, 2018). Lastly, as seen in Chapter Five, there is potential to reduce conflict between separating parents and reach child-led agreements with which children are satisfied by including authentic children's voices in the parental discussion of arrangements for children.

Given this, the next question becomes *how* we can move towards achieving a children's rights approach to family justice, noting the barriers to CIM discussed in Chapter Three. Our principal argument in this context is that incorporation of the UNCRC into UK domestic law should be the goal in the longer term. This would, in itself, acknowledge children as rights-bearing subjects with interests distinct from their parents (Dimopoulos, 2021).

Yet, this depends on garnering political will, which is not guaranteed. To lay a strong foundation for incorporation and for it to work effectively, we must first achieve both a conceptual and cultural shift away from the parental autonomy norm in mediation and wider family dispute resolution towards one that recognizes children as people and development actors, not just passive objects. We see no reason why steps towards this shift could not be taken immediately, particularly through expanding CIM and adopting the Lundy model approach (Lundy, 2007: 933). We see CIM as an important vehicle that is available and can be adapted in the short term to embed an article 12 approach. If developed appropriately, this would, based on our evidence, enhance the process for families and, at the same time, demonstrate how a children's rights framework might well be an asset rather than a threat within the wider family justice system. These steps could also be aided in the short to medium term by some statutory, procedural and practical changes which would help move the law, process and practice towards acceptance of the value of the UNCRC principles in resolving post-separation child arrangements within our family justice system.

Our concluding chapter now draws together the themes and arguments made in the preceding chapters to consider the conceptual, legal and practical changes needed to build a family justice system that has mediation at its centre, in this context, but which is fully compliant with article 12 UNCRC. By this, we mean a system that takes children's information, consultation and participation rights seriously, and ensures young people can exercise appropriate agency in practice, achieving a balance not present within the prevailing parental autonomy discourse.

Conceptual changes: parental autonomy versus children's rights

Based on our findings about the barriers to uptake of CIM in Chapter Three, we consider there needs to be a key conceptual change to understandings of autonomy and rights in how family mediation in the child arrangements context is constructed. We have seen in Chapter One that family mediation is perceived and regulated as an adult enterprise, which must always be child-focused (albeit through parent-filtered accounts). It can be child-inclusive, but only if both parents agree. Thus, normatively, it is parental autonomy (including understandings of parental 'rights') which is the cornerstone of family mediation (Roberts and Moscati, 2020). This, in practice, can often mean that child arrangements become the parents' lowest common denominator for agreement, which may or may not coincide with the child's wishes or, indeed, their best interests, an issue which the young people in this study felt was a grave injustice. While in some senses, the current approach to encouraging private ordering aligns with rights under article 8 of the European Convention on Human Rights, guaranteeing respect for private and family life, it is ignoring not only UNCRC General Comment No. 12, which explicitly extends article 12 rights to the mediation process (2009: para 32), but also the Council of Europe's 2003 recommendation that children should be heard in mediation (Council of Europe Recommendation, 2003: para 4). Given the strength of feeling by young people in this and other studies, our first recommendation is that the normative understandings of autonomy and private ordering within family mediation must be re-envisioned to include children's views in the decision-making process within mediation *as the default*. To be clear, that is not to advocate that young people's views will or should always prevail, but rather that they are gathered directly from the children and taken seriously as part of the dispute resolution considerations, balancing them against other important considerations about how to further their best interests. As noted in Chapter One, family decision-making is, by its very nature, relational, where relationships and caring obligations place constraints on the exercise of individual autonomy by family members (Fineman, 2004; 2013; Wallbank and Herring, 2014). That is to say that the exercise of autonomy by any family member will often have unacceptable repercussions for other members, which in practice do or should act as a brake on its use. Therefore, autonomy is not a pure concept in this context but, at best, a relational one. While, arguably, this is understood within mediation as between the adult parents, unless CIM is undertaken, parents are free *not* to inform, consult or take account of the wishes and interests of their children, other than through such parental narratives as are presented in the process. Children, as we have seen, quite often have no information, let alone autonomy or agency, as they go through parental separation, whichever out-of-court process is chosen by their parents. This, in turn, adds to their inherent vulnerability and deprives them of their article 12 rights.

Based on our research evidence, we consider that parental autonomy should not 'trump' young people's article 12 rights to be heard when parents engage in mediation following separation in this way.

Relational family autonomy in CIM

Instead, given the imperative of serving children's wellbeing during the difficult period of parental separation, we suggest that mediation of child arrangements could and should become a process which recognizes children's desire for information and gives them appropriate agency regarding decisions which affect their lives and futures, respecting their rights ahead of any incorporation of the UNCRC into domestic law. This can be achieved by adapting and reframing the parental autonomy discourse within the family mediation process to balance it against children's article 12 rights. We suggest it is reconceptualized to embed a notion of 'relational family autonomy', which would extend a role in collective decision-making in mediation beyond alignment of parental views to directly include their children's views in that decision, where appropriate. This would reflect and acknowledge the relationship and tension between the rights of parents and children, as articulated in articles 12 and 5 UNCRC. Article 5 in fact requires parents to provide guidance to enable their children to exercise their rights in line with their evolving capacities. Similar to the 'Gillick' principle, it envisages that as children mature and grow in knowledge, the parents' direction and guidance will transform 'into reminders and advice and later to an exchange on an equal footing' (UNCRC General Comment No. 12, 2009: para 84). Thus, the weighting of children's views should reflect that approach which would be explained by the CIM mediator facilitating the parental agreement. Based on our findings, we suggest an enhanced approach to CIM could be a useful trailblazer to test how incorporating UNCRC articles 5 and 12 might be done successfully. Child arrangement decisions would be based on whole family consultation, where children wish to be informed and participate, unless unsafe, shifting practice norms. Although child consultation is undertaken separately from the parents, such decisions would no longer be seen as the preserve of parental discussion alone. While mechanisms for understanding how this would be achieved in an age-appropriate way, acknowledging children's evolving capacities and their development from 'becomings' to 'beings' (Freeman,

2010; Tobin, 2013) are discussed later, CIM would become the normative model for mediation providing it was safe for those involved. For children capable of forming their own views, this would repurpose CIM as a vehicle through which children's article 12 rights were fulfilled and remove the situation where children's views are too often constructed as adult narratives to serve adult interests (Smithson et al, 2015). This approach would also mirror the meaning of 'relational autonomy' in the healthcare context where the concept describes 'interpersonal decisional making ... [where] most seriously ill patients do not utilize solely their own care preferences, but also factor in the care preferences of their loved ones in clinical decision-making' (Fuller et al, 2022: 1, drawing on Zhang and Siminoff, 2003; see also Walter and Ross, 2014).

Reconceptualizing the purpose of child-inclusive mediation

Our findings point to a lack of consensus between mediators on the purpose of CIM and a discrepancy between the views of the relationship professionals, mediators, parents and young people concerning the purpose. If, as suggested, a relational family autonomy principle was accepted, it would reconceptualize the purpose of CIM through what would, in effect, be a children's rights framework, resolving the confusion.

The Family Mediation Council (FMC) should take the lead in redefining the purpose of CIM. It has, as yet, no Code of Practice for CIM, and clearly articulating to parents (and children) the purpose of CIM will build confidence in the process (Brown and Campbell, 2013: 196). Based on our findings that CIM, where practised well, largely coincides with Lundy's call for children to have 'space', 'voice, 'audience' and 'influence' (Lundy, 2007: 933), we now go on to explore what this could mean if appropriate changes were made to re-envision mediation practice in child arrangement disputes to follow the CIM model as the default, adapting this to the requirements of the UNCRC. Appendix III reproduces a checklist for child participation developed to help organizations working with and for children and young people to ensure article 12 compliance. The checklist has been adopted by the Republic of Ireland's Department of Children and Youth Affairs to ensure that 'children have the space to express their views; their voice is enabled; they have an audience for their views; and their views will have influence' (Department of Children and Youth Affairs, 2015: 22). We would suggest that this could be a useful framework for the FMC against which to judge article 12 compliance of its reimagined CIM offer.

Let us now turn to the legal and practical elements of realizing a children's rights framework in England and Wales.

Legal and procedural changes: towards a children's rights framework

Achieving an enhanced article 12-compliant CIM service will require a raft of legal, procedural and practical changes to how CIM is conceptualized and practised. This will require cooperation and goodwill across the FMC member organizations and between the FMC and policy makers. Achieving such compliance for the family justice system as a whole will involve greater challenges. However, we suggest that the changes needed to make CIM article 12 compliant can lay the foundations and help change the culture for the longer-term development of a comprehensive children's rights-based family justice system.

Incorporation of the UNCRC

The most obvious legal change to achieve a children's rights framework would be the incorporation of the provisions of the UNCRC into domestic law. The government stressed its commitment to promote and implement the UNCRC across the UK in its response to the Family Justice Review in 2012 (MoJ and DfE, 2012b: 10). Yet over a decade on, this commitment remains rhetoric rather than reality. In 2021, the UN Committee asked the UK to explain the measures it has taken to '[b]ring its domestic legislation into line with the Convention and ensure that the principles and provisions of the Convention ... are directly applicable and justiciable under domestic law, particularly in England' (UN Committee on the Rights of the Child, 2021). As we have seen in Chapter One, its dissatisfaction with progress was expressed again in 2023, and steps to facilitate children's rights to express views and access meaningful participation called for (UNCRC Committee, 2023: paras 23(a) and (b)). These calls are also made against a backdrop of the Westminster government's recent Supreme Court victory, which successfully challenged Scotland's attempts to do just that, albeit on constitutional grounds.[1] To date, Wales alone in the UK has succeeded in incorporating provisions of the UNCRC into its domestic law (Rights of Children and Young Persons (Wales Measure 2011)), although not in a way which can be enforced by the courts, as recommended by the UNCRC (Doyle et al, 2017). The Scottish government remains committed to implementing an amended version of the Scotland (Rights of the Child (Incorporation)) (Scotland) Bill 2021, which would incorporate the UNCRC. However, this is likely to remain a much longer-term goal in England.

As signalled earlier, we support the incorporation of the UNCRC into UK domestic law in all UK nations, including the provisions of article 12 as the key legislative goal. Once embedded in our law, it would ensure that children's rights are taken seriously and change the culture in and beyond legal discourse. As Lundy et al (2013: 463) observed, '[i]ncorporating the UNCRC into domestic law provides a platform from which other legal and non-legal measures develop. Positive

---

[1]   Reference by the Attorney General and the Advocate General for Scotland – United Nations Convention on the Rights of the Child (Incorporation) (Scotland) Bill [2021] UKSC 42.

consequences of how children's rights are perceived and implemented in practice, that would be difficult to achieve through other means, flow from incorporation'.

This is borne out by UNICEF's study of implementation in 12 countries (Lundy et al, 2012), which confirmed that in countries which had incorporated (Belgium, Norway and Spain) children were better understood as rights holders, which in turn created a culture of respect for children's rights and returned positive benefits beyond the legislative procedure itself. In Ireland, constitutional reform to include a children's rights provision was achieved in 2015. Although adoption of the provisions of the UNCRC itself has been piecemeal, this approach has been found to have been gradually transformative in building a culture that respects, protects and fulfils children's human rights (Forde and Kilkelly, 2021).

We therefore propose that pending incorporation of the UNCRC into UK law or other wholesale reform, alternative ways should be found to lead a transformation in practice so that children's existing international law rights are recognized and implemented appropriately when parents separate in line with UNCRC expectations.

Alternative routes to realizing UNCRC rights on parental separation

Given that children already have UNCRC rights, including their rights under article 12, as a matter of international law, finding ways to help realize them in the mediation context should be possible. Family mediation does have a CIM pathway and its own FMC Standards Framework. Although we have demonstrated both the benefits experienced by young people and identified the barriers to uptake of CIM, we have also indicated where CIM as a practice does and does not achieve compliance with article 12 UNCRC. If the FMC could itself, or working with others, start the drive to take action to address the barriers and improve compliance, this would be an important step in the right direction. While, as discussed later, there are measures which we suggest the FMC and mediation community could take on their own initiative, including underpinning mediation with a relational *family* autonomy approach to agreeing child arrangements and embedding Lundy's model within CIM, we take the view that some domestic legislative changes would add weight to the call for transition towards both a re-envisioned CIM process and a change of approach to child arrangements within wider family dispute resolution practices. Let us first consider what this might entail.

Statutory change

We propose that relatively small domestic legislative changes could be adopted to aid the focus on children's rights under article 12. This could change the approach both in and out of court to resolving child arrangement disputes. No mandatory provision governs children's participation in domestic private child law proceedings. Where the parents agree, there is no statutory obligation to consult the children at all since the welfare checklist in section 1(3) of the Children Act (CA) 1989, which requires the court to consider the ascertainable wishes and feelings of the child in light of their age and understanding, applies only to contested section 8 *proceedings* (Freeman and Lowe, 2021: 173). Aldridge (2017) argues that while Part 2 of article 12 gives young people the right to participate in administrative processes (such as mediation), the opportunity to be heard must be offered 'in a manner consistent with the procedural rules of national law', which makes it difficult for young people to exercise their right when they have no legal standing or agency. Meaningful participation for young people in decision-making in England and Wales is unlikely to be achieved until the procedural rules in this jurisdiction, backed by statutory requirements, provide mechanisms to ensure that young people's article 12 rights will be upheld and enforced where needed.

To achieve this, we suggest some relatively simple changes to primary legislation. Had section 12(2)(a)(iii) of the Family Law Act 1996 been implemented, practitioners would have had a duty to inform clients of the importance of considering the child's welfare, wishes and feelings, alongside the other welfare criteria listed. However, in the new landscape of private ordering, which encourages parental agreement, practitioners of any sort do not necessarily have a role in child arrangement disputes. Yet if parental autonomy is to be replaced with the principle of relational family autonomy in mediation, we suggest a duty similar to that envisaged under the 1996 Act be placed on mediators at the Mediation and Information Assessment Meeting (MIAM). This would go hand in hand with stricter enforcement by courts of the expectations of attendance at the MIAM for assessment of the parents' suitability to mediate before taking child arrangement issues to court (s 10(1) Children and Families Act 2014; Family Procedure Rules (FPR) Practice Direction 3A; FPR Practice Direction 12B). This would likely expand the number of parents attending MIAMs and, therefore, being informed about their children's article 12 rights and the opportunity of consulting the child through CIM, with the potential benefits for children.

A further duty could be placed on separating parents to discuss the proposed child arrangements with their children and seek their views. This could perhaps be included in the CA 1989 as part of their parental responsibility (s 3) or separately included elsewhere. Parental responsibility is defined (s 3(1)) as 'all the rights, duties, powers, responsibilities and authority which by law a parent of a child has in relation to the child and his property'. An explicit clarification that this includes a parental duty to consult and a responsibility to take seriously children's views on matters affecting their lives in an age-appropriate way, including on child arrangements following parental separation, would fulfil this aim. This would do no more than give a statutory basis to the obligations under articles

5 and 12 UNCRC while underlining the break with parental autonomy and ensuring that children are informed about the situation. This should in no way place children in a position of having to choose which parent's view they support but rather ensure that there is a discussion which informs children about the opportunity and rights they have to be informed and to express their own views independently. In Scotland, Children (Scotland) Act 1995, section 6, already obliges a person reaching any major decision which involves fulfilling a parental responsibility to

> have regard so far as practicable to the views (if he wishes to express them) of the child concerned, taking account of the child's age and maturity, and to those of any other person who has parental responsibilities or parental rights in relation to the child (and wishes to express those views).

As we have seen, young people are usually already aware of the difficulties that their parents are experiencing, and their preference, based on this study, is that they would welcome the opportunity to be included in the conversation about their future in an age-appropriate way. This will ensure they feel respected and give them a beneficial outlet, which we have seen is important to their wellbeing.

Another possible statutory change we would propose is extending the welfare principle in section 1(1) CA 1989. This makes the child's welfare the court's paramount consideration *in court proceedings* determining any question concerning the child's upbringing. In our view, this principle should also extend to mediation (and, in principle, to arrangements negotiated by parents by other means) so that any agreement reached is checked against the child's wishes and feelings and their wider welfare as set out in the welfare checklist (section 1(3) CA 1989). As we have seen, the child's welfare is not necessarily the paramount consideration in mediation, where parental agreement is the driving force within the process and mediators are facilitators to, rather than architects of, that agreement. While promoting the child's welfare is part of the professional code of practice (FMC, 2018: para 5.7.1), as noted in Chapter One, this is not an enforceable duty. Given the shift to resolving child arrangement disputes in mediation rather than court wherever possible, it seems crucial to safeguard children's welfare within this process to the same extent as in court proceedings. Indeed, given that UNCRC article 3 makes the child's welfare the 'primary' (not 'paramount') consideration in this context, such a change might be considered a valuable clarification after incorporating the Convention into UK domestic law.

Practical changes: towards a children's rights framework

Several practical steps could be taken in the short to medium term both to increase awareness of CIM and children's existing international rights under the UNCRC more generally in the context of post-separation child arrangements, helping to achieve a cultural shift in public attitudes and professional practice. We set out a range of larger and smaller scale suggestions to realize this aim.

Child-inclusive mediation awareness and education about children's rights-changing expectations

This research shows that parents and young people have low awareness of CIM before engaging in mediation. Awareness that children have article 12 rights was virtually non-existent among parents and children in our study and was not always appreciated by mediators. We therefore recommend that alongside relationship education in schools, there should be a public awareness campaign to raise the profile of CIM and increase awareness of children's right to be informed and consulted when parents separate. This should highlight the availability and benefits of CIM, as well as the expectation that children should be involved, to the extent which is appropriate given their age and level of understanding, in making child arrangements when parents agree these directly or use non-court processes (PD12B: 4.4). This will help to embed the cultural shift away from a paternalistic and parental autonomy approach towards acceptance that children have views and rights to have them considered in this context.

As we have seen in Chapter Three, relationship education is considered by young people to be a good place for all children to learn about relationships. Citizenship education is also a forum for young people to understand their rights, including under the UNCRC. The authors, working with the National Youth Advocacy Service (NYAS) and the National Association of Child Contact Centres (NACCC), have, as a follow-on from this research, designed lesson plans and videos for both primary and secondary school-aged children aimed at introducing young people to their article 12 rights under the UNCRC. These materials have been quality assured by the PSHE Association and the Association for Citizenship Teaching, where possible, and explain and signpost ways to get information and access support, including about CIM, should parents separate (Family Solutions Children's Group, 2023: 18). Education is one major avenue to increasing rights awareness among children and in line with the views of our young people participants in this study, this is being made available to all children in appropriate lessons, not just those whose parents are separating.

A universal child-inclusive mediation offer to children and parents

The message from the young people we spoke to in interviews and focus groups was that there should be a universal offer to the children of parents in mediation of an optional meeting with the mediator. This accords with the recommendation of the recent, JUSTICE (2022). This may cause some consternation within the mediation community. While accepting that 'the starting point in child-inclusive mediation is that their direct involvement should be routinely and actively considered at an early stage', Allport (2020: 196) questions how the suggestion of meeting children without parental consent might sit with parents whom she refers to as mediators' 'primary client group'. She rightly raises concerns about how children could be invited without parental consent and the risk that parents might refuse to return to mediation. However, suppose an offer of CIM became the norm, a cornerstone of mediating child arrangements just as much as voluntary participation and confidentiality are at present, and it is framed that way to the parents. In that case, the evidence from this research is that some of these concerns are likely to melt away. As a minimum, it would provide an opportunity for children to have an outlet to express their views to an independent third party, which they see as helpful and important to their wellbeing. Young people's article 12 rights are not qualified rights. Only a universal offer to young people providing them with a meaningful forum to express their views, whichever non-court process their parents choose, would meet our international obligations.

Murch (2018) suggests that there may be a case to argue that young people should be invited to the MIAM. We take the view that the MIAM performs an important screening function for suitability for mediation, and needs to be performed before a child is invited into the process. However, we suggest that as part of the screening process, the mediator should be required to consider whether the case is suitable for CIM and if there are no contra-indications, but the parents are reluctant, or think the child might be reluctant, there should be an invitation to the child to a pre-meeting for them to find out about CIM. Where CIM is deemed unsuitable, the mediator and parents should consider how the child is to be given the opportunity to express their views or have their information and support needs met, for example, through a referral to counselling, other online or local support services, or pastoral support within schools as appropriate for the child. The relational family autonomy approach we propose will ensure that the needs of the children will be central and considered explicitly from the outset. It is for the child to then decide which support, if any, they would like to take up. The evidence from this research points to young people appreciating the offer of support, even if it is not taken up, as it reinforces that their needs are central to decision-making.

Child-friendly information

A child rights-based approach to arrangements on parental separation must start with the availability and accessibility of child-friendly information for young people (Stalford et al, 2017: 208). This, as Stalford et al (2017) further explain, should give children what they want to know – practical and procedural information about what will happen; foundational rights-based information about their rights and status; confirmation of their agency; and space and opportunity within the process which will enable them to use the information given and to assert their rights.

In child arrangement cases following the MIAM, assuming that parents are not screened out as being unsuitable for CIM, the mediator should, in our view, be able to contact the child directly to invite them to a consultation meeting per their right to express a view, should they wish to. At the same time, child-friendly, age-appropriate information about CIM would be provided. The Family Mediators Association has, for example, produced *A Young Person's Guide to Mediation* in conjunction with young people, and a link to such a guide should be made easily available to the child by text, e-mail or post, as is their preferred method of communication. Sources of support such as ChildLine or NYAS could also be provided. Links to the videos available for this purpose, such as those used with the lesson plans (Family Solutions Children's Group, 2023: 18), would also be useful to some parents and children. Once the child consultation meeting and mediation are concluded, we suggest feedback on how the child's views have been listened to (or why they have not) should be given to the child sensitively to ensure that the checklist for 'influence' outlined in Appendix III is met. Managing children's expectations of the process will be crucial, and signposting to further help at this stage would also be important.

Development of the process should, we suggest, be co-created with children in local areas and representative groups such as the Family Justice Young People's Board. This would fully align with Stalford et al's view that 'participation both depends upon and facilitates children's understanding of the information they receive and the processes they are going through and, in turn, enables them to have a meaningful stake in any decisions involved' (Stalford et al, 2017: 212).

Enhancing mediator training and skills: reframing the offer

A crucial element of an expanded CIM service is enhanced mediation training to embed the skills and children's rights mindset undoubtedly needed within the new culture and practice we call for. Some progress has already been made, but our study identifies specific aspects that need to be improved to successfully transition to a CIM default model of mediating child arrangements disputes, in addition to proposed changes to the Code of Practice discussed separately in what follows.

The obligatory mediation training for all mediators, alongside that required for CIM practitioners, provides the opportunity to radiate the message to all mediators that children are rights-bearers whose need for age-appropriate information and agency must be respected. The use of the MIAM to consider the benefits for children's wellbeing in exercising their article 12 rights and to encourage parents in appropriate cases to guide and help children understand and exercise those rights in the way foreseen in article 5 UNCRC would be an important focus of enhanced CIM training.

Our findings suggest that *how* the mediator frames the offer of CIM to the parents (and the children) is critical to uptake rates. Douglas et al (2000: 59) report that when the practitioner suggests they talk to their child, the parent generally follows this advice. Our evidence concurs with this finding. Framing the offer positively to the parents, alluding to the benefits for children's wellbeing and the fact that children have the right to be heard in matters that affect their lives, will help stress the positive aspects of CIM for many children. How any individual child responds will vary, but framing the offer as an opportunity for their child to receive information and uphold their right to participate in decision-making in a separate child consultation meeting with the mediator is likely to be received positively by parents. When constructed as a child's right, it immediately becomes more difficult for either parent to be the one to deny their child the opportunity. A skilled mediator explaining the benefits to children will help allay understandable protective and often well-intentioned paternalism so that the child themself is given agency. Crucially, therefore, mediator training needs to embed this approach.

Enhancing mediator training and skills: understanding the additional benefits

Our research evidence suggests that some parents and practitioners have a limited view of hearing from children, consulting the child to break an impasse. In contrast, young people spoke of benefits far beyond progressing the case. While acknowledging that a duality of purpose may exist, making the importance of being heard to a child's wellbeing the primary purpose is likely to assist the mediator in overcoming any 'kneejerk' parental reluctance. Mediator training should embed the relational family autonomy approach as a norm and ensure that mediators have the requisite skills to engage positively with parents and children about the value of CIM, rather than seeing it as a last resort. Training should enhance understanding of not only children's article 12 rights, but also the benefits of giving children a voice in and of its own right, based on research, an approach which seems critical to ensuring that CIM is truly child-centred. This, in turn, will help mediators to help parents reach the right decision for the child's welfare, after seriously considering their wishes, and reduce the cases where these elements are unjustifiably ignored to ensure parental agreement is reached. That is not to place the mediator in the same position as a judge, but would change the dynamic of the tripartite CIM conversation, so that the power is less skewed, and children are not just objects of the dispute. Throughout the book, we have used Lundy's characterization of the elements needed to realize children's article 12 rights as a lens to understand how well or otherwise CIM embodies the requirements of giving children 'space', 'voice', audience' and 'influence' (Lundy, 2007: 933) and we think would be a useful tool in mediator training. The Lundy Pathway Model in Appendix II could be used first to understand the elements needed within a children's rights framework for CIM. Lundy's Voice Model Checklist for Participation in Appendix III would then give a practical way of training mediators to check that these elements had been implemented successfully in their CIM sessions.

As the culture towards a children's rights framework within family justice system shifts, we would hope that professional training of lawyers and judges would also incorporate such a checklist into their own practice in child arrangement cases to ensure children's perspectives are embedded meaningfully.

Addressing structural barriers

As Dimopoulos (2021: 443) convincingly argues, a child's substantive rights to decisional privacy are ineffective without procedural rights to facilitate meaningful participation in decision-making processes about matters that affect them. Unless the structural and cultural barriers we have identified are addressed, children's substantive right to meaningful participation in decision-making when parents separate will not be upheld. Bestowing rights without effective remedies by which to exercise those rights does children a disservice (Freeman, 2010; Ferguson, 2013). We now consider what could be done.

Costs and legal aid

Addressing the structural barriers to CIM, such as costs, is imperative. We endorse calls by the Family Solutions Group (2020: para 91), the JUSTICE Report (2022: para 3.72) and the Voice of the Child Advisory Group Report (2015: Recommendation 33) for the government to take steps to put the funding of CIM onto a proper footing. Just as (before the introduction of the £500 voucher scheme) the first mediation session was funded regardless of means to encourage participation in mediation, we recommend that at least one session of CIM for each child of the family is funded by the Legal Services Commission, where the child has expressed a desire to meet with the mediator. Echoing the findings of McIntosh et al (2008), our research illustrates mental health and wellbeing benefits to young people who speak to the mediator with whom their parents are meeting. This alone should justify the expense. The research also shows that CIM can assist parents in reaching an agreement in mediation, thereby avoiding the financial and emotional cost to the parents (and their children) of court proceedings and the cost of proceedings to the public purse. This may go some way to relieving the significant backlogs in the family court, where private law cases took an average of 45 weeks to reach a final order in 2022 (Ministry of Justice, 2023). Once the inclusion of child consultation within the mediation process is normalized, data collection over cases nationally could form part of the FMC's survey practice and its effects could also be monitored within legal aid mediation starts and court statistics.

Reframing the approach to hearing from and listening to young people in a way that acknowledges their evolving capacities and participatory rights (Tobin, 2015), as we have suggested, could, therefore, also help to overcome the structural barrier of costs. Given that our international obligations to hear from children should be addressed meaningfully, the question becomes *how*, not *whether*, this is funded at public expense, particularly when wellbeing and conflict reduction benefits are factored into any cost–benefit analysis.

While our research has focused on CIM, young people's right to be heard extends to whichever non-court process their parents engage in to try to resolve matters. The government must implement funding mechanisms to ensure that children's voices are heard in other non-court processes such as solicitor negotiations, collaborative law or arbitration. The government has placed an expectation on parents (and the professionals supporting them) that they will ensure that children are involved in the decision-making when parents separate (PD12B: 4.4). It is fitting that for those parents who are eligible, funding mechanisms should be in place to meet the cost of involving children in the non-court process used. We endorse the recommendation of the JUSTICE Report that consideration is given to how child consultation can be financially incentivized in privately paying non-court processes (JUSTICE, 2022: para 3.77).

Code of Practice: embracing the child-inclusive mediation challenge

If young people's substantive participatory rights are to be upheld resolutely and consistently, this will require a fundamental change in culture in the mediation community. Under the heading of 'welfare of children', the FMC's Code of Practice dedicates only five short sub-sections to hearing from children. As noted, the FMC has a separate Code of Practice for online mediation but not for CIM. We would invite the FMC to urgently review the position and devise a Code of Practice for CIM. We would suggest that the Code adopts the wording of CA 1989, section 1(1) so that the child's welfare becomes the 'paramount consideration' in mediation as it is in court proceedings. The current requirement that the mediator should 'have particular regard' to the child's welfare and 'encourage the parents' to focus on the child's needs as well as their own falls short of an article 12 compliant process.

To give young people both the 'space' and the 'voice' required of an article 12 compliant process (Lundy, 2007: 933), where there is a sibling group, the Code of Practice should contain a requirement that CIM must include an individual element with each child to allow the child to discuss matters that they may not feel comfortable discussing in front of their siblings. The comments mentioned later regarding the existing code should, we recommend, be included in any standalone Code of Practice for CIM.

Code of Practice: age of the child

The FMC's Code of Practice requires that '[a]ll children and young people aged 10 and above should be offered the opportunity to have their voices heard directly during the Mediation, if they wish' (FMC, 2018: para 6.6.1). We agree with the JUSTICE Report that an arbitrary presumptive age threshold for hearing from children risks the converse presumption that children under the threshold do not need access to their participatory rights (JUSTICE, 2022: para 3.65). Arbitrary age thresholds also ignore the evolutionary capacity of children recognized by article 5 and risk tokenistic approaches to participation (McCall-Smith, 2021). We recommend that the Code of Practice be amended to remove the reference to any presumptive age. This would help to bring about the culture change we believe is required to ensure that mediation practices comply with our international obligations. The UN Committee on the Rights of the Child has emphasized that 'age alone cannot determine the significance of a child's views', but instead, the child's capacity to form a view must be 'assessed on a case-by-case examination' (UNCRC General Comment No. 12, 2009: para 29). Removal of the age restriction in the Code of Practice would ensure that mediators specifically consider hearing from *all* children where appropriate. Children's right to give their views under article 12 is unqualified. All children enjoy the right; it is the weight placed upon those views which is qualified and must be considered in light of a child's age and maturity.

Perhaps to avoid being too prescriptive, the FMC's Code of Practice (2018) is silent on how the offer to have their voice heard should be made to young people and does not include any requirement that the mediator records how or whether an offer is made. We would endorse the call of the Family Solutions Group that mediators should be required to record annual statistics on the number of children invited to a consultation; the number of CIMs carried out each year; and where the mediator proposed CIM but it did not go ahead, whether the mother, father and/or child declined (Family Solutions Group, 2020: para 95). Additionally, as the Family Solutions Group Report recommends, a reason should be recorded should the mediator decide that CIM is inappropriate. This would help the mediator to address their mind to how the child, in this case, might be facilitated to participate. This, combined with removing the age restriction mentioned earlier, would require mediators to think creatively about how to include the children's views in an age-appropriate manner rather than potentially dismissing participation based on age alone.

Family Mediation Council Standards Framework: feedback to young people

Feedback to parents of their children's views is an integral part of an effective CIM process, yet feedback to the child on how their views were considered and the weight that was placed upon them is largely overlooked. Currently, within judicial processes, efforts to render the justice process more 'child friendly' have tended to focus on procedures and processes for children *pre*-decision (Stalford and Hollingsworth, 2020: 1031). The position is similar in mediation. The FMC Standards Framework (2014: 6.4j) requires mediators to 'offer and arrange ongoing support and further meetings with the child or young person as appropriate'. However, it does not require feedback to the child on the decisions made or the extent to which their feedback shaped the decisions. Yet, General Comment No. 12 (2009: para 45) provides, '[s]ince the child enjoys the right that her or his views are given due weight, the decision maker has to inform the child of the outcome of the process and explain how her or his views were considered'. While the parents may be the ultimate 'decision makers' in mediation, in addition to anything that each parent may convey to the child, there should be at least some short oral feedback from the mediator to the child outlining the outcome and how their views were considered. To ensure compliance, we suggest that there should be a requirement that mediators keep a record of when and how this was done. Monitoring how the child's participation influenced the outcome safeguards against tokenistic participation, making it uncomfortable for the adults involved to hear but then ignore the child's views (Lundy, 2007: 939).

Next steps

We conclude that we must take our international obligations much more seriously to facilitate and give due weight to young people's right to express their views freely, should they wish to. Ideally, this ethos should permeate the approach to all post-separation child arrangements made in and out of court. Article 12 provides that State Parties 'shall assure' the right of the child to express her or his views freely. As General Comment No. 12 reminds us, ' "Shall assure" is a legal term of special strength, which leaves no leeway for State parties' discretion' (UNCRC

General Comment No. 12, 2009: para 19). The obligation on State Parties to ensure that mechanisms are in place to, first, solicit and, second, give due weight to children's views when parents separate is a strict one. As we have seen, CIM has much to offer children and their separating parents. As an initial step, revisioning CIM through a children's rights framework would help address some barriers to greater uptake of the process and help implement safeguards for participating children. It is to be hoped that the FMC and wider family mediation community are ready to embrace this opportunity to take the lead. Making CIM normative within mediation practice would begin to constructively challenge the appropriateness more widely of a policy dominated by the neoliberal belief that 'autonomy' for parents in decision-making following separation is unreservedly good (Fineman, 2013). It would recognize young people's evolving capacities and participation rights (Tobin, 2015). Critically, it would also provide a meaningful remedy to children whose parents engage in mediation, minimizing the risk, identified by Freeman (2007), that rights for children become merely symbolic. Assessment of a child's best interests under article 3 must include respect for the child's article 12 right to express his or her views freely; the two are inextricably linked (UNCRC General Comment No. 12, 2009: para 74; UNCRC General Comment No. 14, 2013: para 43).

In child arrangement disputes, introducing CIM as a default process that recognizes and respects the dynamics of a relational family autonomy principle would really begin to put children at the heart of family dispute resolution. In time, this should act to change the prevailing culture and pave the way to wider acceptance of a children's rights framework in our family justice landscape. However, incorporation of the UNCRC into domestic law throughout the UK needs to remain the ultimate goal to ensure the legal entrenchment of children's rights, finally endowing them with a recognized legal status in domestic as well as international law. Surely, UK children deserve no less.

APPENDIX I

The *Healthy Relationship Transitions (HeaRT)* Research Study: Project Design and Methods

Design background

The *Healthy Relationship Transitions (HeaRT)* study was a distinct strand of a wider interdisciplinary research project, *Transforming Relationships and Relationship Transitions with and for the Next Generation*, which was funded by the Wellcome Trust as a Beacon Project of the Wellcome Centre for Cultures and Environments of Health at the University of Exeter (Grant Ref: 203109/Z/16/Z). It was conducted in 2020 and 2021 and used qualitative methods adjusted due to the COVID-19 restrictions operating at the time.

The objectives for the project as a whole were to:

- Explore the desired content and outcomes of relationship education (RE) from the perspectives of young people.
- Support young people to become resilient adults capable of making positive choices and maintaining happy, health-promoting, intimate relationships.
- Reduce the adverse consequences of parental conflict on child (and parental) health by exploring the value of promoting greater child consultation through child-inclusive mediation (CIM) to improve wellbeing and agency for young people whose parents separate.

The project comprised two strands: *Healthy Relationship Education* (*HeaRE*), led by Exeter Medical School colleagues, Newlove-Delgado and Benham-Clarke, and *HeaRT*, led by the authors. The *HeaRE* strand focused on the role of RE in schools and explored the desired content and outcomes of RE from young people's perspectives, including their views on whether parental separation should be addressed as part of the curriculum in RE. The *HeaRE* strand methods and findings are not relevant to this book's focus and are not directly discussed, save where they inform aspects of the *HeaRT* study. Full details of *HeaRE* are published elsewhere (Barlow et al, 2022; Benham-Clarke et al, 2022a; 2022b).

The *HeaRT* strand of the project was focused on practice, experiences and views relating to CIM. Its aim was to reduce the adverse consequences of parental conflict on child and parental health by collecting and analysing evidence on whether more child consultation through greater CIM uptake could improve wellbeing and agency for young people in the context of parental separation. The findings from both strands came together to suggest ways to support young people to become resilient adults, capable of making positive choices and maintaining happy, health-promoting, intimate and family relationships, with greater understanding of transitions into and out of such relationships. In accordance with the co-creation approach of the project, all findings from both strands were presented for critique and discussion at an online workshop with a combined youth panel comprising young people participants from both *HeaRE* and *HeaRT* in February 2021, which helped challenge and confirm our thematic analysis (Barlow et al, 2022).

The *HeaRT* study: research ethics approach and approval

Research ethics approval was applied for *HeaRT* in accordance with the University of Exeter research ethics procedures and was approved on 20 December 2019 (Ethics approval no. 201920–017 [adults] and 201920–040 [young people]). Informed consent was obtained from all participants, and child-friendly information sheets about the project were provided for our child participants. The names of all participants were anonymized, and any names referred to in this book are pseudonyms. Adults were ascribed surnames to distinguish them from young people. As we were interviewing parents and siblings from the same families, there was a risk to internal confidentiality – the risk that those inside a group may identify other group members (Tolich, 2004: 101). To avoid jigsaw identification of family groups, young people were given first names only, adults who shared a surname were given different surnames and the gender of siblings was anonymized.

The *HeaRT* study: purposive sampling and data collection methods

The *HeaRT* study was conducted in two phases. The first focused on collecting data from relationship experts and family mediators. The second on members of separated families who had undertaken CIM.

To understand the CIM process and models of good and bad practice more thoroughly, first a reflexive workshop was held with 11 CIM mediators and three family justice professionals from the Ministry of Justice, Cafcass and the Family Justice Young People's Board (FJYPB) to pool knowledge and expertise about the process, including identifying their collective understanding of the risks and benefits of the process to separating parents and their children. The workshop, and the first two focus groups with the FJYPB (discussed in what follows), took place in February 2020, shortly before the first COVID-19 lockdown, and were conducted face-to-face. All subsequent focus groups, workshops and interviews undertaken for the *HeaRT* study were conducted online.

In order to understand how older children can learn skills needed to identify healthy and unhealthy relationships and cope better with relationship transitions across the life course, including from an intact to a separated family, we used qualitative semi-structured telephone interviews with ten relationship professionals (psychotherapists, counsellors and researchers; seven women and three men) purposively sampled for their known expertise in supporting couple relationships or counselling young people following parental separation. For the *HeaRT* strand, their views on the wellbeing benefits (and risks) of giving young people a voice in the decision-making when parents separate, and the role that CIM might play in this, were explored. We report the findings from the *HeaRT* strand in Chapter Two.

Next, we conducted two focus groups with ten members of the FJYPB to consider their views on the risks and benefits of CIM. The first focus group comprised those aged 11–16, and the second, 16 years and over. We then conducted two mixed-age focus groups with a total of eight FJYPB members to gather their views on young people's information and support needs following parental separation. An interview was also conducted with a young adult family law campaigner using the same focus group schedule. All had experienced parental separation. Three groups included a mix of genders and one contained girls only. The groups had a mix of ethnic backgrounds.

Following this, we undertook qualitative semi-structured interviews with a sample of 20 family mediators, CIM qualified for an average of 16 years. All were Family Mediation Council (FMC)-accredited, and all FMC member organizations were represented. Recruitment was undertaken in layers. First, we re-approached CIM-qualified mediators identified in the earlier *Mapping* study in 2012 (Barlow et al, 2017b). Here, we found many mediators were CIM qualified yet were reluctant to undertake CIM due to a lack of confidence and/or parental objections to their child participating (Barlow et al, 2017b: 77). This approach enabled a judgement of whether their CIM practice (and confidence in the process) had increased, declined or remained stable over the intervening ten years.

The additional mediators were recruited through adverts in the FMC and its member organizations' newsletters. This resulted in a sample of 17 women and three men, reflecting the female bias within the family mediation profession.

Our parent sample comprised 12 parents (five fathers and seven mothers) each of whom we interviewed using a semi-structured interview approach to allow comparability within the sample as well as space to capture the individual narrative. These parents had all engaged an FMC-accredited mediator and, as with the mediator sample, all FMC member organizations were represented. Some parents had been legally aided; others had paid privately. We asked parents to score their conflict level with the other parents out of ten and triangulated their score with their description of the conflict in interview. Seven parents self-identified as high-conflict disputes (scoring eight or higher out of ten). The others were classified as 'mid-range' conflict, with scores of between five and seven. We also interviewed 20 young people (nine girls and 11 boys, aged 9–19). We interviewed one or more children plus one or both of their parents in all but two cases, with 12 different families represented. Recruitment of parents and children was through contacts with FMC-accredited mediators or the FJYPB.

The post-separation child arrangements prior to engaging in the CIM process for the 12 family situations within our sample varied as summarized in Table AI.1.

Finally, in July 2021, we brought together an engaged research panel of 21 relationship and education professionals with one now-adult family justice campaigner to discuss the findings and next steps.

The HeaRT study: approach to analysis

The semi-structured interviews and focus groups were recorded, transcribed and analysed using Braun and Clarke's (2006) six phases of thematic analysis and inductive approach in NVivo with a codebook per sample developed by Ewing.

Table AI.1: Child arrangements prior to mediation

Pre-mediation arrangement	Number of cases in category
Father primary carer	3
Mother primary carer	5
Maternal grandparents primary carer	1
Parental shared care	2
Nesting arrangement[*]	1
Total	**12**

Note: * A 'nesting' arrangement is where the children stay in the family home, and the parents move around them, rather than the children having to visit different homes.

A blind double-coding process was employed to ensure consistency of the thematic approach, with two research team members coding one interview from each sample. We ran a coding comparison query in NVivo for each interview double coded. Any codes with a Kappa co-efficiency score of ≤0.75 (0.75 and over being considered 'very good', Fleiss et al, 2003) were discussed to agreement and codes refined before coding the remaining interviews to ensure inter-coder reliability and demonstrate the trustworthiness of the findings.

In line with the research objectives, we sought throughout to capture the experiences of CIM from the perspective of different actors, identify the benefits and risks of CIM as well as the barriers and facilitators to achieving engagement in the CIM process by parents and children. We present the findings in Chapters Two to Five inclusive.

APPENDIX II

Lundy's Conceptual Model of the United Nations Convention on the Rights of the Child, Article 12 Inclusion

Figure AII.1: Lundy's conceptual model of the United Nations Convention on the Rights of the Child, article 12 inclusion

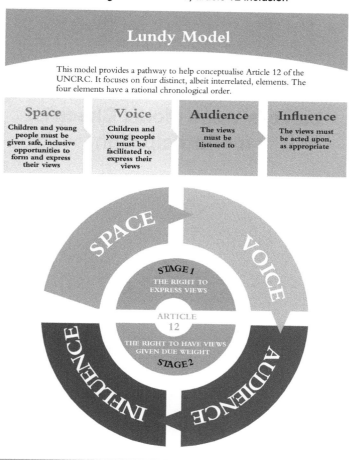

Source: Reproduced with the kind permission of the Department of Children, Equality, Disability, Integration and Youth, Government of Ireland from the Department of Children, Equality, Disability, Integration and Youth's *Participation Framework: National Framework for Children and Young People's Participation in Decision-making* (2021: 15).

APPENDIX III

Lundy's Voice Model Checklist for Participation

Figure AIII.1: Lundy's voice model checklist for participation

Everyday Spaces Checklist

This checklist is designed as a guide to help you ensure that children
and young people have a voice in decision-making. It can be applied
in many everyday situations including in classrooms, hospitals, childcare
settings, child and youth services, youth and sports clubs, youth projects,
arts and creative initiatives and other spaces.

Please do not use this checklist for developing policies, plans, services, programmes,
governance, research and legislation – use the Planning Checklist on page 18.

**Please make sure that the ways you involve children and young people
in decision-making are age-appropriate and accessible for all,
whether in person or online.**

SPACE
* How can children and young people feel safe to express their views?
* Have you allowed enough time to listen to and hear their views?
* How do you make sure that all children and young people are heard?

VOICE
* How are children and young people provided with the support they need to give their views and be heard?
* How can they raise the things that matter to them?
* How are they offered different ways of giving their views?

INFLUENCE
* How will children and young people know how much influence they can have on decisions?
* How will you give them feedback?
* How will you share with them the impact of their views on decisions?
* How will you explain the reasons for the decisions taken?

AUDIENCE
* How do you show that you are ready and willing to listen to children and young people's views?
* How do you make sure they understand what you can do with their views?

Source: Reproduced with the kind permission of the Department of Children
and Youth Affairs from Department of Children and Youth Affairs (2015) *National
Strategy on Children and Young People's Participation in Decision-making, 2015–
2020*, Dublin: Government Publications, figure 3, p 22.

References

Al-Alosi, H. (2018) 'Will somebody please think of the children?! Child focused and child inclusive models in family dispute resolution', *Australian Dispute Resolution Journal*, 29(1): 8–20.

Aldridge, J. (2017) 'Introduction to the issue: "Promoting children's participation in research, policy and practice"', *Social Inclusion*, 5(3): 89–92.

Allport, L. (2020) 'The voice of the child in family mediation', in M. Roberts and M. Moscati (eds) *Family Mediation: Contemporary Issues*, London: Bloomsbury, pp 181–202.

Barlow, A. (2017) 'Rising to the post-LASPO challenge: How should mediation respond?', *Journal of Social Welfare and Family Law*, 39(2): 203–22.

Barlow, A. and Ewing, J. (2020) *An Evaluation of 'Mediation in Mind': Final Report*, Exeter: University of Exeter.

Barlow, A., Ewing, J., Hunter, R. and Smithson, J. (2017a) *Creating Paths to Family Justice Briefing Paper and Report on Key Findings*, Exeter: University of Exeter.

Barlow, A., Hunter, R., Smithson, J. and Ewing, J. (2017b) *Mapping Paths to Family Justice: Resolving Family Disputes in Neoliberal Times*, London: Palgrave.

Barlow, A., Ewing, J., Benham-Clarke, S. and Newlove-Delgado, T. (2022) *Transforming Relationships and Relationship Transitions with and for the Next Generation: The Healthy Relationship Education (HeaRE) and Healthy Relationship Transitions (HeaRT) Project Report and Key Findings*, Exeter: University of Exeter.

Barlow, A., Hunter, R. and Ewing, J. (2024) 'Mapping paths to family justice: Resolving family disputes involving children in neoliberal times', in A. Hellner, A. Kaldal and T. Mattsson (eds) *Children in Custody Conflicts Disputes: Matching Legal Proceedings to the Problem*, Cham: Palgrave Macmillan, pp 107–27.

Bell, F. (2016) 'Barriers to empowering children in private family law proceedings', *International Journal of Law, Policy and the Family*, 30(3): 225–47.

Bell, F., Cashmore, J., Parkinson, P. and Single, J. (2012) 'Choosing child-inclusive mediation', *Australasian Dispute Resolution Journal*, 23(4): 253–64.

Bell, F., Cashmore, J., Parkinson, P. and Single, J. (2013) 'Outcomes of child-inclusive mediation', *International Journal of Law, Policy and the Family*, 27(1): 116–42.

Bell, F., Cashmore, J. and Harman, J. (2021) 'Australia', in W. Sharma, M. Freeman, N. Taylor and M. Bruning (eds) *International Handbook on Child Participation in Family Law*, Cambridge: Intersentia, pp 89–102.

Benham-Clarke, S., Ewing, J., Barlow, A. and Newlove-Delgado, T. (2022a) 'Learning how relationships work: A thematic analysis of young people and relationship professionals' perspectives on relationships and relationship education', *BMC Public Health*, 22(2322): 1–11.

Benham-Clarke, S., Roberts, G., Janssens, A. and Newlove-Delgado, T. (2022b) 'Healthy relationship education programmes for young people: Systematic review of outcomes', *Pastoral Care in Education*, 1–23.

Braun, V. and Clarke, V. (2006) 'Using thematic analysis in psychology', *Qualitative Research in Psychology*, 3(2): 77–101.

British Academy (2022) *Reframing Childhood: Final Report of the Childhood Policy Programme, July 2022*, London: British Academy.

Brown, T. and Campbell, A. (2013) 'Parents, children and family relationship centres: what's working?', *Children Australia*, 38(4): 192–7.

Brown, W. (2006) 'American nightmare: Neoliberalism, neoconservatism and de-democratization', *Political Theory*, 34(6): 690–714.

Butler, I., Scanlan, L., Robinson, M., Douglas, G. and Murch, M. (2002) 'Children's involvement in their parents' divorce: Implications for practice', *Children and Society*, 16(2): 89–102.

Butler–Sloss, E. (1988) *Report of the Inquiry into Child Abuse in Cleveland 1987*, London: HMSO.

Carson, R., Dunstan, E., Dunstan, J. and Roopani, D. (2018) *Children and Young People in Separated Families: Family Law System Experiences and Needs*, Melbourne: Australian Institute of Family Studies.

Cashmore, J. and Parkinson, P. (2008) 'Children's and parents' perceptions on children's participation in decision making after parental separation and divorce', *Family Court Review*, 46(1): 91–104.

Cashmore, J., Parkinson, P., Weston, R., Patulny, R., Redmond, G., Qu, L., Baxter, J., Rajkovic, M., Sitek, T. and Katz, I. (2010) *Shared Care Parenting Arrangements since the 2006 Family Law Reforms: Report to the Australian Government Attorney-General's Department*, Sydney: Social Policy Research Centre, University of New South Wales.

Council of Europe Recommendation (2003) *Family Mediation and Gender Equality* No. 1639.

Daly, A. (2018a) *Children, Autonomy and the Courts: Beyond the Right to be Heard*, Leiden: Brill/Nijhoff.

Daly, A. (2018b) 'No weight for due weight: Children's autonomy principle in best interest proceedings', *International Journal of Children's Rights*, 26(1): 61–92.

Dennison, G. (2010) 'Is mediation compatible with children's rights?', *Journal of Social Welfare and Family Law*, 32(2): 169–82.

Department of Children, Equality, Disability, Integration and Youth (2021) *Participation Framework: National Framework for Children and Young People's Participation in Decision-making*, Dublin: Government Publications.

Department of Children and Youth Affairs (2015) *National Strategy on Children and Young People's Participation in Decision-making, 2015–2020*, Dublin: Government Publications.

DfE (Department for Education) (2019) *Relationships Education, Relationships and Sex Education (RSE) and Health Education Statutory Guidance for Governing Bodies, Proprietors, Head Teachers, Principals, Senior Leadership Teams, Teachers*, London: Department for Education.

Diduck, A. (2014) 'Justice by ADR in private family matters: Is it fair and is it possible?', *Family Law*, 44: 616–19.

Diduck, A. and Kaganas, F. (2012) *Family Law, Gender and the State* (3rd edn), Oxford: Hart.

Dimopoulos, G. (2021) 'A theory of children's decisional privacy', *Legal Studies*, 41(3): 430–53.

Dimopoulos, G. (2022) *Decisional Privacy and the Rights of the Child*, Abingdon: Routledge.

Douglas, G., Murch, M., Scanlan, L. and Perry, A. (2000) 'Safeguarding children's welfare in non-contentious divorce: Towards a new conception of the legal process?', *The Modern Law Review*, 63(2): 177–96.

Doyle, M., Harris, J., Millership, L. and Shepherd, J. (2017) *State of Children's Rights in Scotland, 2017*, Scotland: Together (Scottish Alliance for Children's Rights).

Dunn, J. and Deater-Deckard, K. (2001) *Children's Views of Their Changing Families*, York: Joseph Rowntree Foundation.

Eekelaar, J. and Maclean, M. (2013) *Family Justice: The Work of Family Judges in Uncertain Times*, Oxford: Hart.

Ewing, J., Hunter, R., Barlow, A. and Smithson, J. (2015) 'Children's voices: Centre-stage or side-lined in out-of-court dispute resolution in England and Wales?', *Child and Family Law Quarterly*, 27(1): 43–61.

Family Solutions Children's Group (2023) *What about Me? A Child's Right to Matter: Report of a Multi-Disciplinary Consultation Exploring the Needs of Children When Parents Separate*. UK: Family Solutions Group. Available at: https://www.familysolutionsgroup.co.uk/a-childs-right-to-matter-2/

Family Solutions Group (2020) *'What about Me?' Reframing Support for Families Following Parental Separation*, Judiciary UK, 12 November. Available at: https://www.judiciary.uk/wp-content/uploads/2022/07/FamilySolutionsGroupReport_WhatAboutMe_12November2020-2-final-2.pdf

Ferguson, L. (2013) 'Not merely rights for children but children's rights: The theory gap and the assumption of the importance of children's rights', *International Journal of Children's Rights*, 21: 177–208.

Fineman, M. (2004) *The Autonomy Myth: A Theory of Dependency*, New York: New Press.

Fineman, M. (2013) 'Equality, autonomy, and the vulnerable subject in law and politics', in M. Fineman and A. Grear (eds) *Vulnerability: Reflections on a New Ethical Foundation for Law and Politics*, Abingdon: Routledge, pp 13–28.

Fineman, M. (2019) 'Vulnerability and social justice', *Valparaiso University Law Review*, 53(2): 341–70.

Fleiss, J., Levin, B. and Paik, M. (2003) 'The measurement of interrater agreement', in W. Shewart, S. Wilks, J. Fleiss, B. Levin and M. Paik (eds) *Statistical Methods for Rates and Proportions* (3rd edn), New York: Wiley, pp 598–626.

FMC (Family Mediation Council) (2014) *FMC Manual Professional Standards and Self-Regulatory Framework, Family Mediation Council, September 2014 (last updated 1 March 2022)*. Available at: https://www.familymediationcouncil.org.uk/wp-content/uploads/2022/05/FMC-Manual-of-Professonal-Standards-Regulatory-Framework-v1.4.1-Updated-1-March-2022.pdf

FMC (Family Mediation Council) (2016) *Code of Practice for Family Mediators, Family Mediation Council (September 2016)*. Available at: https://www.familymediationcouncil.org.uk/wp-content/uploads/2016/09/FMC-Code-of-Practice-September-2016-2.pdf

FMC (Family Mediation Council) (2018) *Code of Practice for Family Mediators, Family Mediation Council (v.1.3, November 2018)*. Available at: https://www.familymediationcouncil.org.uk/wp-content/uploads/2018/11/FMC-Code-of-Practice-v1.3-November-2018.pdf

FMC (Family Mediation Council) (2017) Family Mediation Survey, Autumn 2017. Available at: https://www.familymediationcouncil.org.uk/wp-content/uploads/2018/01/Family-Mediation-Survey-Autumn-2017.pdf

FMC (Family Mediation Council) (2019) Family Mediation Survey, 2019. Available at: https://www.familymediationcouncil.org.uk/wp-content/uploads/2020/01/Family-Mediation-Survey-Autumn-2019-Results.pdf

REFERENCES

Forde, L. and Kilkelly, U. (2021) 'Incorporating the CRC in Ireland', in U. Kilkelly, L. Lundy and B. Byrne (eds) *Incorporating the UN Convention on the Rights of the Child into National Law*, Cambridge: Intersentia, pp 177–202.

Fortin, J., Hunt, J. and Scanlan, L. (2012) *Taking a Longer View of Contact: The Perspectives of Young Adults Who Experience Parental Separation in Their Youth*. Project report, School of Law, Brighton.

Freeman, M. (2007) 'Why it remains important to take children's rights seriously', *The International Journal of Children's Rights*, 15(1): 5–23.

Freeman, M. (2010) 'The human rights of children', *Current Legal Problems*, 63(1): 1–44.

Freeman, M. and Lowe, N. (2021) 'England and Wales', in W. Sharma, M. Freeman, N. Taylor and M. Bruning (eds) *International Handbook on Child Participation in Family Law*, Cambridge: Intersentia, pp 171–84.

Fuller, T., Hendrick, J. and Beck, A. (2022) 'Fast fact and concepts #439: Undue influence vs relational autonomy in clinical decision-making', *Journal of Palliative Medicine*, 25(6): 996–7.

Gilmore, S. (2017) 'Use of the UNCRC in family law cases in England and Wales', *The International Journal of Children's Rights*, 25(2): 500–18.

Guggenheim, M. (2007) *What's Wrong with Children's Rights*, Cambridge, MA and London: Harvard University Press.

Hanna, A. and Lundy, L. (2021) 'Children's voices', in C. Tomas, G. Trevisan, M. Leote de Carvalho and N. Fernandes (eds) *Key Concepts on Sociology of Childhood*, Braga: Uminho Editora, pp 465–8.

Herring, J. (1999) 'The Human Rights Act and the welfare principle in family law: Conflicting or complementary?', *Child and Family Law Quarterly*, 11(3): 223–36.

Herring, J. (2017) 'Commentary on *Re A (Conjoined Twins)*', in H. Stalford, K. Hollingsworth and S. Gilmore (eds) *Rewriting Children's Judgements: From Academic Vision to New Practice*, Oxford: Hart Publishing, pp 257–63.

Hollingsworth, K. and Stalford, H. (2017) 'Towards children's rights judgements', in H. Stalford, K. Hollingsworth and S. Gilmore (eds) *Rewriting Children's Judgements: From Academic Vision to New Practice*, Oxford: Hart Publishing, pp 53–85.

Hunter, R. (2017) 'Inducing demand for family mediation – before and after LASPO', *Journal of Social Welfare and Family Law*, 39(2): 189–202.

JUSTICE (2022) *Improving Access to Justice for Separating Families*, London: JUSTICE.

Kaganas, F. (2017) 'Justifying the LASPO Act: Authenticity, necessity, suitability, responsibility and autonomy', *Journal of Social Welfare and Family Law*, 39(2): 168–88.

Kay-Flowers, S. (2019) *Childhood Experiences of Separation and Divorce: Reflections from Young Adults*, Bristol: Bristol University Press.

Lansdown, G. (2001) *Promoting Children's Participation in Democratic Decision-Making*, Innocenti Insights no. 6. Florence: UNICEF Innocenti Research Centre.

Lansdown, G. (2005) *The Evolving Capacities of the Child*, Innocenti Insights no. 11. Florence: UNICEF Innocenti Research Centre.

Lansdown, G. (2011) *Every Child's Right to be Heard: A Resource Guide on the UN Committee on the Rights of the Child General Comment No.12*, London: Save the Children UK on behalf of Save the Children and UNICEF.

Lansdown, G. (2019) *Conceptual Framework for Measuring Outcomes of Adolescent Participation*, New York: United Nations Children's Fund (UNICEF).

Lansdown, G. (2022) 'Article 5: The right to parental guidance consistent with the evolving capacity of the child', in Z. Vaghri, J. Zermatten, G. Lansdown and R. Ruggiero (eds) *Monitoring State Compliance with the UN Convention on the Rights of the Child. Children's Well-Being: Indicators and Research*, vol 25, Cham: Springer, pp 117–24.

Law Society (2010) *Family Law Protocol* (3rd edn), London: Law Society Publishing.

REFERENCES

Law Society (2023) 'Children left in limbo by family courts crisis', press release, The Law Society, 1 August.

Lee, N. (2001) *Growing Up in an Age of Uncertainty*, Buckingham: Open University Press.

Lundy, L. (2007) ' "Voice" is not enough: Conceptualising Article 12 of the United Nations Convention on the Rights of the Child', *British Educational Research Journal*, 33(6): 927–42.

Lundy, L., Kilkelly, U. and Byrne, B. (2012) 'Incorporation of the United Nations Convention on the Rights of the Child in Law: A comparative review', *International Journal of Children's Rights*, 21(3): 442–63.

Lundy, L., Kilkelly, U., Byrne, B. and Kang, J. (2013) *The UN Convention on the Rights of the Child: A Study of Legal Implementation in 12 Countries*, Belfast: UNICEF and Queens University.

Lundy, L., Tobin, J. and Parkes, A. (2019) 'Article 12: The right to respect for the views of the child', in J. Tobin (ed) *The UN Convention on the Rights of the Child: A Commentary*, Oxford: Oxford University Press, pp 397–434.

Maclean, M. and Eekelaar, J. (2016) *Lawyers and Mediators: The Brave New World of Services for Separating Families*, Oxford: Hart Publishing.

Mant, J. (2022) *Litigants in Person and the Family Justice System*, Oxford: Hart Publishing.

McCall-Smith, K. (2021) 'Entrenching children's participation through UNCRC incorporation in Scotland', *The International Journal of Human Rights*, 27(8): 1–24.

McIntosh, J. and Long, C. (2006) *Children Beyond Dispute: A Prospective Study of Outcomes from Child Focused and Child Inclusive Post-Separation Family Dispute Resolution, Final Report*, Melbourne: Family Transitions Pty Ltd/La Trobe University.

McIntosh, J., Wells, Y., Smyth, B. and Long, C. (2008) 'Child-focused and child-inclusive divorce mediation: Comparative outcomes from a prospective study of postseparation adjustment', *Family Court Review*, 46(1): 105–24.

MoJ (Ministry of Justice) (2015) *Final Report of the Voice of the Child Dispute Resolution Advisory Group*, London: Ministry of Justice.

MoJ (Ministry of Justice) (2020) *Assessing Risk of Harm to Children and Parents in Private Law Children Cases Final Report*, London: Ministry of Justice.

MoJ (Ministry of Justice) (2023) *Family Court Statistics Quarterly: October to December 2022*, GOV.UK, 30 March 2023.

MoJ (Ministry of Justice) and DfE (Department for Education) (2012a) *The Government Response to the Family Justice Review: A System with Children and Families at its Heart*, February 2012, Cm 8273.

MoJ (Ministry of Justice) and DfE (Department for Education) (2012b) *The Government Response to the Family Justice Review: A Guide for Children and Young People, June 2012*. Cm 8273, Norwich: TSO (The Stationery Office).

Murch, M. (2018) *Supporting Children when Parents Separate: Embedding a Crisis Intervention Approach within Family Justice, Education and Mental Health Policy*, Bristol: Bristol University Press.

Neale, B. (2002) 'Dialogues with children: Children, divorce and citizenship', *Childhood*, 9(4): 455–75.

Neale, B. and Flowerdew, J. (2007) 'New structures, new agency: The dynamics of child–parent relationships after divorce', *The International Journal of Children's Rights*, 15(1): 25–42.

Norgrove, D. (2011) *Family Justice Review*, London: Ministry of Justice, the Department for Education and Welsh Government.

O'Quigley, A. (2000) *Listening to Children's Views: The Findings and Recommendations of Recent Research*, York: Joseph Rowntree Foundation, York Publishing Services Ltd.

Parkinson, L. (2020) *Family Mediation* (4th edn), Bristol: Jordan Publishing.

Parkinson, P. and Cashmore, J. (2008) *The Voice of a Child in Family Law Disputes*, Oxford: Oxford University Press.

Reece, H. (2003) *Divorcing Responsibly*, Oxford: Hart Publishing.

Roberts, M. (2014) *Mediation in Family Disputes: Principles of Practice* (4th edn), London: Routledge.

Roberts, M. and Moscati, M. (2020) 'Introduction', in M. Roberts and M. Moscati (eds) *Family Mediation: Contemporary Issues*, London: Bloomsbury, pp 1–10.

Rudd, B., Ogle, R., Holtzworth-Munroe, A., Applegate, A. and D'Onofrio, B. (2015) 'Child-informed mediation study follow-up: Comparing the frequency of relitigation following different types of family mediation', *Psychology, Public Policy, and Law*, 21(4): 452–7.

Saini, M. (2019) *The Voice of the Child in Family Law: Exploring Strategies, Challenges, and Best Practices for Canada*, Ottawa: Department of Justice.

Sikveland, R. and Stokoe, E. (2016) 'Dealing with resistance in initial intake and inquiry calls to mediation: the power of "willing"', *Conflict Resolution Quarterly*, 33(3): 235–54.

Smart, C. (2004) 'Equal shares: rights for fathers or recognition for children?', *Critical Social Policy*, 24(4): 484–503.

Smart, C. and Neale, B. (1999) *Family Fragments?* Cambridge: Polity Press.

Smithson, J., Barlow, A., Hunter, R. and Ewing, J. (2015) 'The "child's best interests" as an argumentative resource in family mediation sessions', *Discourse Studies* 17(5): 609–23.

Stalford, H. and Hollingsworth, K. (2020) ' "This case is about you and your future": Towards judgments for children', *Modern Law Review*, 83(5): 1030–58.

Stalford, H., Cairns, L. and Marshall, J. (2017) 'Achieving child friendly justice through child friendly methods: Let's start with the right to information', *Social Inclusion*, 5(3): 207–18.

Stewart, J. (2007) 'The mixed economy of welfare in historical context', in M. Powell (ed) *Understanding the Mixed Economy of Welfare*, Bristol: Policy Press, pp 23–40.

Symonds, J., Dermott, E., Hitchings, E. and Staples, E. (2022) *Separating Families: Experiences of Separation and Support*, London: Nuffield Family Justice Observatory.

Tobin, J. (2013) 'Justifying children's rights', *The International Journal of Children's Rights*, 21: 395–441.

Tobin, J. (2015) 'Understanding children's rights: A vision beyond vulnerability', *Nordic Journal of International Law*, 84(2): 155–82.

Tobin, J. and Varadan, S. (2019) 'Article 5: The right to parental direction and guidance and consistent with a child's evolving capacities', in J. Tobin and P. Alston (eds) *The UN Convention on the Rights of the Child: A Commentary*, Oxford: Oxford University Press, pp 159–85.

Tolich, M. (2004) 'Internal confidentiality: When confidentiality assurances fail relational informants', *Qualitative Sociology*, 27(1): 101–6.

UNCRC Committee (2021) *List of Issues prior to Submission of the Combined Sixth and Seventh Reports of the United Kingdom of Great Britain and Northern Ireland*. CRC/C/GBR/QPR/6-7. Published 04 March 2021.

UNCRC Committee (2023) *Concluding Observations on the Combined Sixth and Seventh Periodic Reports of the United Kingdom of Great Britain and Northern Ireland*, adopted by the Committee at its ninety-third session (8–26 May 2023). Published 22 June 2023.

UNCRC General Comment No. 12 (2009) *The Right of the Child to be Heard*, CRC/C/GC/12. Fifty-first session, UN Committee on the Rights of the Child (CRC).

UNCRC General Comment No. 14 (2013) *On the Right of the Child to Have His or Her Best Interests Taken as a Primary Consideration (art. 3, para. 1)*, CRC/C/GC/14. Sixty-second session, UN Committee on the Rights of the Child (CRC).

Varadan, S. (2019) 'The principle of evolving capacities under the UN Convention on the Rights of the Child', *The International Journal of Children's Rights*, 27(2): 306–38.

Voice of the Child Advisory Group (2015) *Final Report*, March 2015. Available at: https://assets.publishing.service.gov.uk/media/5a7f9 6cced915d74e33f75c9/voice-of-the-child-advisory-group-rep ort.pdf

Walker, J. and Lake-Carroll, A. (2014) 'Hearing the voices of children and young people in dispute resolution processes' in *Report of the Mediation Task Force*, June 2014. Available at: https://www.just ice.gov.uk/downloads/family-mediation-task-force-report.pdf

Wallbank, J. and Herring, J. (2014) 'Vulnerabilities, care and family law', in J. Wallbank and J. Herring (eds) *Vulnerabilities, Care and Family Law*, London: Routledge, pp 1–21.

Walter, J. and Ross, L. (2014) 'Relational autonomy: moving beyond the limits of isolated individualism', *Paediatrics*, 133(Supplement 1): 16–23.

Zhang, A. and Siminoff, L. (2003) 'The role of the family in treatment decision making by patients with cancer', *Oncology Nursing Forum*, 30(6): 1022–8.

Index